AF595830

Wakefield Press

The Road Less Travelled

Born and raised in Adelaide, Heather Caddick has had a diverse career spanning kindergarten teaching to stockbroking and investment. She has always been passionate about voluntary work, encompassing wildlife and humanitarian causes in Africa. When she is not travelling, she lives in Adelaide with her husband, Alfie. This is her second book.

The Road Less Travelled

(and being curious)

Heather Caddick

Wakefield
Press

Wakefield Press
16 Rose Street
Mile End
South Australia 5031
www.wakefieldpress.com.au

First published 2016

Edited by Julia Beaven, Wakefield Press
Designed by Liz Nicholson, designBITE
Typeset by Wakefield Press

National Library of Australia Cataloguing-in-Publication entry

Creator:	Caddick, Heather, 1944– , author.
Title:	The road less travelled (and being curious) / Heather Caddick.
ISBN:	978 1 74305 454 3 (hardback).
Subjects:	Caddick, Heather, 1944– .
	Caddick, Heather, 1944– – Travel.
	Women adventurers – Australia – Biography
	Adventure and adventurers – Anecdotes.
Dewey Number:	920.72

Contents

Preface vii

Sea Adventures on the '*Guglielmo Marconi*' (1966) 1

The Golden Girls – An Irish Odyssey (1966) 11

Lifting the Veil on Arabia (1983) 17

Melodramas in Malawi (2010) 23

Swedish Language School, Studies with Refugees (2011) 31

Winter in Turkey (1989) 38

Riding Istanbul's Magic Carpet (1989) 45

Outback South Australia (2014) 51

Brindisi by Train (1983) 58

Ethiopia – Harar and Hyenas (2008) 65

Catholics and Protestants in Belfast (1968) 72

Zanzibar (2005) 79

Dhow Drifting in Oman (2013) 86

Pamukkale, Konya and Cappadoccia by Bus (1989) 91

Etosha and Tracking Desert Elephants (2015) 99

Epilogue 107

Preface

Two roads diverged in a wood, and I
took the road less travelled by

ROBERT FROST

A nursery song about the bear climbing over a mountain to see what he could see has been at the core of my wanderlust. Each mountain climbed or road less travelled triggers a curiosity to turn the next corner and discover more.

The maze of travel adventures in this book blends the wonders of nature with humanitarian causes and frivolous escapades with cultural insights; it lifts the veil on the Middle East and Turkey, tells of studying Swedish with refugees in Sweden, attending an IRA rally before the onset of hostilities in Ireland, and of wildlife encounters in Africa.

By using fearlessness, charm and humour in foreign lands, I have found that walls of suspicion can collapse in a sea of goodwill and fun.

My dream is of a global village working as one, to balance the problems of wildlife and habitats with human life, and to preserve this balance as a heritage for our children's children.

Heather Caddick, 2016

Sea Adventures on the 'Guglielmo Marconi' (1966)

I must go down to the sea again
To the lonely sea and sky
And all I ask is a tall ship
And a star to steer her by

JOHN MASEFIELD

After years of planning and saving, here we are boarding the *Guglielmo Marconi*, elegantly parked dockside at Outer Harbor in Adelaide. The wharf is milling with crowds of onlookers and families farewelling young Australians like us, embarking on working holidays overseas.

It is late afternoon, and the band is playing 'The Carnival is Over', the Seekers latest hit song, as we direct porters to take our trunks to the hold. Suitcases for the voyage are sent to our cabin, brimming with flowers from friends wishing us well.

Caroline opts for the top bunk, I choose to sleep at floor level. We have a pencil-slim shower recess with a basin and loo. There is no porthole, but as we don't intend to spend our days cabin-bound, we are happy. My mother runs her fingers over the dressing table, checking for dust, whilst our fathers organise a champagne toast. A blast from the ship's horn tells them to disembark, we are about to sail.

Streamers cascade down from the decks to the wharf as passengers prepare for slow goodbyes, each holding a streamer attached to a loved one on shore. Excitement is building, with much shouting and waving to crowds of relatives gathering together on the wharf. We assemble at the deck railings to see Mary slowly unravelling one kilometre of stockings. She has spent months knotting them together, our last link between ship and shore.

'Don't forget to take the pill!' Caroline's mother shouts from the wharf, causing hilarity from family and friends. But she is referring to seasickness tablets, not the newly liberating contraceptive pill.

Three more blasts from the ship's horn and we can now hear and feel the rumble of powerful engines as the *Marconi* edges away from the dock, the band playing 'The Carnival is Over' yet again and colourful streamers floating down to the sea.

Mary's stocking chain still links us to shore, finally dropping to the water as we sail from the harbour into open sea.

The next three days of sailing are so rough that we are cabin bound with seasickness. The *Marconi* pitches through the waters of the Great Australian Bight, one of the world's most turbulent waterways. I lie on my bunk and watch a brunch coat sway from side to side on a door hook and contemplate flying home to Adelaide from Perth. I can understand thoughts of jumping overboard to end the nausea. Caroline and I alternate sick posts, from the cabin basin to the outside deck. We have not yet sighted the dining room, nor have we met any other passengers.

Day three dawns, and mercifully there is calm water and no wind, just a gentle breeze that teases the white caps of the ship's wake. We both stagger to the top deck to stretch out on

wooden benches, allowing the sun to warm and soothe us. We are not alone. Weak passengers, pallid and battle scarred by the past two days are also seeking refuge from their cabins.

We meet Mary, Nicholas, Robbie, Anne, Jenny, Michael and Peter. All are heading to Europe to work and travel. The age demographic on the *Marconi* seems to be predominantly between twenty and thirty years, as we are in the second-class sector of the ship. First class is the domain of older and wealthier passengers.

We are lying just below the Captain's bridge and the bridge's small deck, where five delicious-looking Italian officers in pristine white uniforms with gold braid are standing at the railings, looking down on us with amusement. There is much posturing and posing with a distinctive air of sophistication, contrasting starkly with our limited exposure to such male beauty in Adelaide.

'They obviously don't get seasick,' I say to Caroline

'No, they are just surveying the talent on board for the voyage,' she replies presciently.

We dock at Perth, where a bevy of my relatives meet us. Once on terra firma, we find our appetites return and there is the hilarity of a family re-union that lasts all day. We are dropped back to the ship for the next leg of our voyage to Singapore, revived and now ready to fully enjoy shipboard life.

The swinging sixties with the contraceptive pill, and all the freedom that this entails, is background to this era Although there is obviously subterranean cabin activity on the *Marconi*, Caroline and I were brought up with the ethic that 'Nice girls don't', well at least not until choosing the marriage path, and to be frank, the idea of starting a committed and meaningful

relationship on board is eons away from my mind. Here we have scores of young people, all hell bent on the ultimate adventure of discovering the world, realising dreams and seeing places heard about since childhood.

Every day we swim, play deck quoits and board games, read, put on plays, laze on deck, plan costume balls and theme-based dinners. There is wine, music and song, and it is the most wonderful fun to be part of a gang of like-minded Australians, from all over our vast land. A committed relationship would spoil the heady freedom, but we enjoy a trail of admirers amongst these new friends, not to mention Italian officers circling, although their presence is restricted to formal dinners and balls.

The Marconi Queen of the Sea Ball is a formal occasion. We gain access to the hold to rummage through our trunks for ball gowns from formal debutante and graduation days in Adelaide, where long gowns made in beautiful fabrics were *de rigueur.* I have even packed my long white kid gloves, and find a shocking pink taffeta dress beaded around the décolletage, and Caroline's Gucci-styled turquoise chiffon gown has a sweetheart neckline and back floating panels of silk.

A buffet dinner begins the celebration, and the glorious presence of uniformed officers just adds to the frisson. The Captain welcomes us all, and the band plays as he sashays onto the dance floor with his buxom and beautiful wife. Everyone is dressed up to the nines, with men in back tie rig, even coat tails are on show. We dance until midnight and the celebrations conclude with a conga line that extends from the ballroom to the stern, around the swimming pool and back to the ballroom. The night sky is a myriad of stars and a full moon plays with the phosphorescence of the wake.

We are now getting to know our fellow passengers and some of their stories, plans and dreams. Sandy is a ski instructor from Falls Creek, en route to Austria where she will spend the winter season instructing and meeting up with her Austrian boyfriend who runs the ski school in Kossen Tyrol. Jenny is from a pastoral family in South Australia and is an outstanding equestrienne. She is heading for Ireland to be a strapper on a horse stud south of Limerick. Nick, a university student in Adelaide, is going home to Singapore, where his parents are in the diplomatic corps. Now he is part of our gang, he wants to continue the voyage with us to Naples.

Caroline and I aim to take our chances in London, where there is ample work on offer. I am planning to work at Australia House as one of the ten 'Golden Girls', who swan around the United Kingdom promoting all things Australia, supervised and chaperoned by the legendary Blair Cook. Caroline will find secretarial work in London to tide her over until her parents arrive in June. Everyone has flexible plans and ideas, with no fear of destitution. Jobs are plentiful, and Australians are highly regarded as competent and hard workers.

We are about to cross the equator. Nick will be King Neptune, and adjudicator for the pool games that must be attended to receive the document marking your successful crossing to the Northern Hemisphere. A board is placed over the pool. Two contenders are blindfolded and must sit astride the board, with a large bowl of spaghetti in the centre. The idea is to feed your opponent spaghetti, and of course, being blindfolded, the trick is to stay balanced. It is almost impossible and we all end up in the pool. After much hilarity, shrieking and dousing we are initiated and receive the document signed by King Neptune to immortalise the crossing.

We enter the Port of Singapore and are met by friends of Caroline's family. The teenage children play host and show us Chinatown and Bugis Street, with the parental directive that Bugis Street, Singapore's famous red light district, is strictly off limits ringing in our ears. Bugis Street is bustling with activity and gaudy flamboyant dressing is on show, worn by a variety of genders. The atmosphere is exciting and non-aggressive, but we do see loud and inebriated American sailors causing a fracas outside one of the clubs. Bugis Street is fascinating, opening our eyes to an underbelly we don't see in Adelaide.

We buy delicious hot spring rolls served on sticks and cooked by street vendors on the pavement, another new experience. Later a family dinner at the Colonial Club overlooking the harbour completes our day on shore, before we are returned to the ship to set sail for Bombay.

There has been a death on board. An elderly passenger has died from a heart attack and the sober announcement is made at breakfast, with a funeral planned to take place the next night. The ship's chaplain will officiate with a funeral mass.

'Let's go to the funeral,' I say to Caroline. 'It will be paying respects to a fellow passenger, but also fascinating to see what they do.'

It is 11 pm and we put black jumpers over our dinner clothes and make our way to the stern of the ship, standing at the back of a small congregation. The chaplain is gowned in white and gold Catholic splendour, and a coffin draped in the Italian flag sits on a bench that meets the stern railing, a gate now open to the sea and the glistening wake. The service is in Latin and Italian, soft music is played and hymns sung. The captain leads a line of officers as pallbearers. They lift the coffin gently,

allowing it to fall to the sea below. The only sound is of the sea and wind, with the starry firmament above lighting the white caps of the vast black ocean.

'What a perfect way to leave this world,' says Caroline. 'It's as if the sea is inviting him to journey to paradise.' The elegance and dignity of this service has a profound effect on us both.

There is excitement and anticipation when Bombay appears on the horizon, and as the *Marconi* docks we can hear, see and smell something entirely different and completely exotic. Indian business colleagues of Caroline's father meet us, and we are shown the sights from the top of a double-decker bus that wends its way through slums and markets teeming with people, strong and weak, rich and poor, and beyond our imagination. We are told of children's bones being broken and left untended so they may appear more pathetic and needy as beggars and earn more money for their parents.

In the meat markets carcasses hooked onto rods above the counter are littered with flies. The butcher slices meat off the carcass for a customer and rolls it in newspaper after haggling over the price. There is a smell of sewerage, heat, spices and sweat, and this morning our conservative Adelaide eyes have been opened in stark amazement at the sights of Bombay.

We are taken to a club for lunch, a colonial bastion of British decorum and tradition, but they thankfully serve wonderful Indian curries, not over-cooked meat and veggies, and we try Bombay duck and other delicacies, gently guided by our hosts.

The Gateway to India proudly stands as a monument to British rule, and nearby the magnificent Taj Mahal Hotel, built with opulent Victorian splendour in 1903, is a perfect place to end our day. Gin and tonics are served in the marble-floored

front bar, where we sink into brass-studded leather club chairs cooled by the gentle swish of ceiling fans.

Our next port of call is Aden, tentatively under British rule, and because of recent terror incidents we are escorted off the ship by British soldiers, who chaperone us for the entire visit. The bazaars are filled with exotic silks and pungent perfume oils but we are more interested in the state of tension here and watch Arabs being frisked for grenades and weapons and notice a strong military presence wherever we go. We return to the ship laden with silk scarves and perfume oils, which are rather sickly to smell in the intense humidity.

The Suez Canal is so narrow we could virtually reach out and touch the camel trains sauntering by on land. Touts and traders gather at Port Said, their small dinghies brimming with goods for sale. They circle the ship, a drawbridge-type platform extending from the hull allowing passengers to deal directly with the traders. It is now nightfall and the noise, smells and chaos is endlessly fascinating as we hang over the ship's rails watching it all.

Giza and the pyramids are a day-long excursion. We soon realise that being tall and blonde is a distinct disadvantage in Egypt, and the day experiencing the exceptional wonder of the pyramids is spent fending off hoards of touts, keen to escort us, or entice us onto their camels for a photograph. They charge an exorbitant fee – which escalates once you mount the beast – and won't let you off the camel until you pay.

We enter the Pyramid of Cheops, and climb a steep and rickety ladder that gains entry to the holy of holies – the actual tomb. I feel a hand wandering up my leg as I climb, and shout and kick with fury. The offender behind me loses his grip on

the ladder and falls to the ground and Caroline, who is waiting her turn to be escorted to the inner sanctum, buckles up with laughter as he rushes past her to escape censure.

We spend the afternoon at the Cairo Museum wandering around mummies and extraordinary relics from ancient Egypt, with a pause for pomegranate tea and sweet and gooey cakes.

Our Mediterranean crossing to Naples is marked by stormy seas with freezing winds sweeping across the sea from the wintry north, and on our final nights aboard the *Marconi* deck chairs and all things moveable are strapped securely to the sides of the ship. Passageways have knotted ropes attached, allowing passengers to safely steer their way as the ship pitches from side to side.

On the final night of dinner and dancing couples veer around the dance floor in sway with the sea, which has mercifully reduced to a gentle roll as the storm subsides. Addresses are exchanged and a *Marconi* reunion in London planned as our gang prepares for disembarking in Naples.

It is dark at 5 pm, with a wintry bite to the air as we dock. The trunks are being dispatched overland to London, and we take one suitcase each for our Eurail pass, where we may board any train, anywhere in Europe, over the next month. Soon we are walking down the gangway, where a taxi driver greets us and the cases are piled into his little Fiat.

'Pensione Napoli, *per favore*,' says Caroline, and our driver takes off with one hand on the steering wheel and one on the horn, punctuating the weaves and turns with a loud toot. We drive through back streets and along a highway then more back streets and finally stop outside Pensione Napoli, parting with a great deal of English money as he rings the doorbell, and in

a flash is gone. The next morning I open the blinds to see the familiar elegant shape of the *Marconi* silhouetted in the early morning light, just five minutes from our *pensione*.

Welcome to Europe, girls!

The Golden Girls – An Irish Odyssey (1966)

The Irish are a race of people for whom psychoanalysis is of no use whatsoever

SIGMUND FREUD

'Now, girls, be at Heathrow 10 am sharp, and the press will meet us on the runway for a shot of you all on the gangway of our plane.'

Blair Cook is preparing us for our first sortie into the world of the Golden Girls, and I am one of ten girls chosen to host trade fairs, exhibitions, the wool secretariat, and major Australian events as part of the Trade Publicity Department of Australia House in London.

'Be sure to wear a hat at the interview,' I had been advised before meeting the legendary Blair, who was rarely without one. I did so and, to my delight, was recruited.

Being director and chaperone of the Golden Girls, Blair has specific requirements, and complete autonomy over whom she chooses. She requires Australian girls, minimum height of five feet six, 'Aussie beach girls' but with education, and what she calls 'background'. These days are emphatically non-politically correct but, dare I say, the impact of ten such advocates in wintry England is instant, with publicity following the team wherever we go, coupled with free press for Australian trade and Australian companies.

We have just emerged from a week's indoctrination at Australia House, including one day spent at the model school that groomed Jean Shrimpton and Twiggy.

We are coached in the art of applying eyeliner and false eyelashes for TV appearances, have lectures on poise and grooming.

The school is situated in Bond Street, and we spill out during lunch to window shop the trends, and take in the sights of this nerve centre of London's pop culture. It is the late sixties, and swinging London is well and truly swinging! Earls Court is crammed with Australians on working holidays, living in less than salubrious bedsits or basement flats, where hungry gas meters require coins for heat, and bread is toasted on radiators. These privations are part of the fun and excitement of being away from home. Plusher apartments are soon gained, as good jobs are easy to attain for Australians.

I have a much-loved aunt and uncle in Harrow and, being childless, they welcome me as a daughter, providing me with a permanent base. The tube is an easy connection to friends and to Australia House in the Strand.

Blair selects an interesting group, and we soon meld into a team, with Georgie, Marg and Gizelle becoming a sub-group of my special friends. Georgie is from outback Queensland, tall and willowy with that risk-taking daring that accompanies the freedom of a childhood spent on a sheep station. She is engaged to Scottish Mike, who must complete another year in the Navy, after which they will marry and return to Australia.

Marg was a secretary in Sydney and planned her escape to London, once she had saved the fare. She has enormous blue eyes and can put on an innocent face. With her sense of the ridiculous she has everyone around her collapsing with laughter.

Gizelle escaped the Communists in Hungary and migrated to Australia, leaving her family in Budapest. She sold stockings in Mark Foys, Sydney, while learning to speak English, and then applied and was recruited by Qantas. Now fluent in four languages, she flew the world for seven years as an airhostess, on their most exotic routes. 'Dizzy Gizzy' suits her personality, and shiny black hair mirrors an animated face that attracts attention and admiration wherever she goes.

Blair continues her briefing with, 'Now, girls, pack your navy suits but wear the mustard, and don't forget your Aage Thaarup hats!' Aage Thaarup was the Queen's milliner at this time and with Blair's love of hats, the perfect choice for her girls. Our mustard suits are meant to emulate wattle, and look very chic. They are made to measure in light merino wool gabardine, with straight skirts and tailored jackets so there will be impact when we are 'en masse'.

Blair greets us at Heathrow looking like the Queen Mother, and fusses over each of us to see that we pass muster. She then orders the Press photographers to follow her as we line the gangway to the cabin door of BOAC's comet. We are flying to Shannon airport in Southern Ireland, and will spend a week in Limerick for Australian Trade Week. Shannon airport is a short flight from London, and the airport bus is soon winding us along narrow lanes in County Clare, through lush country-side with dry-stone walls fencing the farms. To me, everything seems to be in miniature, with tiny cottages, small paddocks and narrow lanes. It's like Gulliver's travels.

Suddenly the bus stops, and it appears the driver has recognised a friend driving a tractor. He gets out of the bus and props himself against a stone wall, lighting a cigarette as they

chat away, and it's a good twenty minutes before he stubs out his third cigarette, waves to the farmer and climbs back into the driver's seat to continue our journey to Limerick.

'This is Ireland, girls!' laughs Blair, highly amused, and we finally arrive at our hotel in the centre of town, where the Australian flag is flying from a flag pole over the hotel entrance, marking Australian Trade week in Southern Ireland.

Corporate trading partners from Australia and Ireland are invited to a reception at the hotel with our ambassador officiating; journalists and local dignitaries will also attend. We are to be hostesses, and mingle, so there is a flurry of unpacking, with the whirr of hairdryers, and our connecting rooms an easy access to much borrowing and lending of forgotten items. It's rather like a school boarding house.

We hear the hotel manager has been phoned and told, that unless he takes down that Union Jack flag the hotel will be bombed. When the caller hears it is an Australian flag for Australia Trade Week, he says, 'Well, that's all right then, all my relatives live in Australia, you can leave it flying, and I'll tell them to hold off on the Molotovs!'

The reception is what one might call a 'knees up'. Drinks flow during speeches, and it seems our ambassador is decidedly the worse for wear. He staggers out with his stoic wife in tow, having tried to goose Gizzy during the official photo shoot. She reacted by planting her stiletto heel firmly on his shoe, and his wince of pain alerted Blair, who smilingly approached him, and stood at his side for the duration of his visit.

The room is awash with Irish charm, and new friendships are being sealed with invitations to see Ireland's wonders. I seem to have an admirer called Malachy, who insists on a date

to drive me to Tralee. I accept, with the riposte that I hope the roses are in bloom.

During the week, we are assigned to small businesses, to meet and greet locals, talk about Australia, and 'Just be yourselves, girls!' says Blair.

'Do you speak English?' and 'How many kangaroos are in your garden?' are frequent questions, but overall, there is friendliness and curiosity, plus the most endearing generosity, with home-made Irish buns delivered every day to the hotel, 'For the Australian girls'.

One afternoon, a parcel is left at the hotel, addressed to me, Heather Goldsmith. The caption reads: Please accept this book of the works of Oliver Goldsmith, Ireland's greatest poet, who must be your forebear, and Ireland, your ancestral home. This anonymous gift was prompted by a photo in the local paper.

Walking across the Shannon bridge on a free afternoon, Georgie and I decide to explore the back streets of Limerick, where the word 'slums' would better describe the living conditions. A television aerial pokes out of a muddy mound, which is in fact a house made from rubble and a few sheets of iron, the muddy tracks crisscrossed with tumbledown cottages huddled close together. We are aware we might appear snoopy, so make a quick retreat to the riverbank and continue in the direction of open fields. (Decades on I realise that this was the area of Frank McCourt's childhood, vividly described in his book *Angela's Ashes*.)

We hear speeches being blared through a megaphone, with cheers and angry tirades as we approach a field and a gathering of around 500 people. We stand at the back to watch. A band gets on stage with three bearded musicians strumming guitars and singing what sounds like an Irish folk song, and it is hard

to get the gist of what is going on until the chorus: 'And we'll blast the bloody British back across the Irish Sea!' followed by resounding cheers and clapping! This is an IRA rally, and we are at the tipping point of what will become a brutal civil war for the next three decades.

'Now, girls, the helicopter will ferry you in threes to Bunratty Castle for the Trade Week farewell dinner,' says Blair. 'We shall get a bus to the heliport, and it's just a ten-minute flight to the castle. Please wear your navy suits, and be careful of the mead, it's fire water!'

It's a limpid evening of muted colours, with wisps of mauve pink clouds in the sunset's trail. We hover over the silvery Shannon estuary in the helicopter, and soon Bunratty Castle appears, like a fable from storybooks, its turrets and battlements bathed in the fading light. The noisy chopper jolts this reverie to the present. Georgie, Marg and I alight, and bend low beneath the spinning rotor blades. We head for the castle entrance across a drawbridge that leads to the Great Hall, resplendent with medieval tapestries. Mead is served in goblets, and I would say this drink of fermented honey is the nectar of the gods, but wisely decline refills, as verbose and mead-fuelled speeches lauding Trade Week are delivered, with the most memorable being from our ambassador, who seems to enjoy mead as much as Irish whisky.

We finally enter a magnificent banquet hall, where sturdy benches border long oak tables, lit with candles and laden with roasts. Irish harps and fiddles are playing, and later a concert of medieval Irish songs puts an indelible stamp on our kinship with Ireland. *The pipes, the pipes are calling* and, like Danny Boy, we shall return.

Lifting the Veil on Arabia (1983)

There are blessings in the desert, where the sky is your ocean, and the crystal silence will uplift you like gospel music

ANNE LAMOTT

We are approaching Dubai and the boys are transfixed by single flames poised above what looks like a line of Bunsen burners, marking the oil wealth of the Emirates as we make our descent to the airport. Toby aged nine and Barney seven have been asleep for hours, head to toe at my feet, bolstered by cushions. This was before more stringent rules for flying with children became mandatory.

Dubai is a jewel of the desert, and this trip was thirty years before its transformation into a hectic Fantasyland of skyscrapers, twirling freeways and almost obscene luxury.

We are visiting my friend Mary, who has established herself here over many years, managing one of Sheik Rashid's companies, which, in such a male culture, is unusual. She is highly respected by local ruling families, and was the only non-Arab woman to attend Sheik Mohammed's wedding party. Mary is tall and wears conservative Western dress. These friendships, with her charm, intelligence and quick wit, ensure she takes pride of place at important events in Dubai.

For centuries, the locals of Dubai were nomadic desert dwellers. With the discovery of oil, their small and largely

illiterate population was able to jump from camels into Maseratis, with instant exposure to the excesses of the Western world.

At this time the Ruler's birthday present to every male turning twenty-one was $50,000 ($200,000 today). To foster Dubai's development the ruling families imported largely British expertise, with the axiom that locals must own fifty-one per cent of the company and have representation on every board.

A British engineering friend of Mary's was headhunted to build a $20 million ($100 million today) canal, from the Persian Gulf to a sheik's palace, built nearby the Abu Dhabi freeway. The sole purpose of this canal was to allow the sheik to moor his multi-million dollar cruiser by the palace, for all to see as they drove by.

Abdullah, Mary's driver, meets us, and his flowing white dishdasha complete with white guthra (head scarf) secured to his head by a black corded circlet gives him stature and elegance. He briskly walks towards us, hand extended to formally greet and welcome us to Dubai. 'Mary has been detained at work, but will be home by the time we arrive,' he says.

We pass an estuary known as The Creek. Locals cross it in *abras*, small wooden boats with bench seating and canvas covers, to reach the Gold Souk and spice and perfume bazaars set in a maze of shop fronts and alleyways. Dhows moored nearby with their brightly painted hulls and furled sails remind us of the Arabian Nights. There are even a few camels tethered together beside a dhow, and beyond is the white and seemingly endless expanse of the Arabian Desert.

It is now nightfall, and minarets are floodlit around statuesque mosques, with deafening calls to prayer ringing out,

aided by megaphones, the sound colliding with calls and tones from nearby mosques.

We settle into Mary's apartment with the help of Goanese houseboy Pedru, and spend the first day exploring the Souks. The Dubai Gold Souk is considered the finest in the Persian Gulf, and is literally laden with gold. Gold is historically prized as a display of wealth, as well as providing a refuge for troubled times, and is sold either as jewellery or by ingots. One alleyway sells only gold coins, including ancient Persian coins, and sovereigns, with Krugerrands being the most sought after as an international currency.

We are in a small jewellery atelier when a local Emirati enters followed by three women covered in black abayas, hijabs covering their heads and gold kid niqabs covering their mouths and noses. Six black eyes are all that's visible. Emirates law allows a man to have three wives, and the tradition rules that his gifts must have exactly the same value for each wife. We watch loud emotion and carry-on over the choice of gold jewellery between these three women. Toby tells me he feels sorry for the husband, he thinks one wife would be enough!

We linger in the Spice Bazaar, enticed by the smell of pungent spices displayed in huge hessian sacks at the door of each shop. Vibrantly coloured saffron is prized and very expensive. Sacks of cloves, cumin, cinnamon, ginger, turmeric and cardamom to flavour coffee are spooned into packets for the customers bustling through the marketplace.

A siesta to escape the heat is a merciful relief, and it's as if a door closes on all activity in Dubai between 2 pm and 5 pm. At around seven the pantomime of life begins once more in the souks and bazaars, with families socialising and children

playing together – and often not gathered up for home until midnight.

Mary joins us for falafels and pomegranate juice as we watch The Creek come to life, the *abras* shunting backwards and forwards and dhows lit up with fairy lights gently sailing by, the smell of spiced barbecued meat wafting across the water.

Pedru is packing a picnic hamper. There is much discussion as to what should go into the pita wraps before chilled vine leaves are layered over them and dates, figs, and some luscious marzipan is added. An esky for cool drinks is neatly packed into the car.

It is Thursday, the beginning of the Arab weekend and always a confusing conundrum to Western business travellers. Mary is driving us to the Buraimi Oasis, which borders Oman and was at the crossroads of ancient trading routes for centuries past. The desert shimmers in the morning light, but the 120-kilometre freeway between Dubai and Al Ain is now 'sprinkler-systemed', so that we are on an emerald-green ribbon of grass and shrubs cutting through the stark white, endless sands of the Arabian Desert.

Before long, mirages can be seen on the horizon as the sun plays tricks on our perspective and we expect to come across a lake or inland sea. Al Ain is a small desert town and we drive through to Buraimi, where enormous date palms announce the oasis, protected by an ancient turreted fort. We park the car and walk with the hamper under the shady shroud of the date palm canopy, listening to the tinkling of water streaming through a system of narrow channels that have been in use since 1000 BC. Fruit and citrus trees and vines flourish, and walled plantations delineate property of the sheiks' and locals' families.

We settle in a clearing, with a picnic rug placed on a cushion

of palm leaves, and begin our feast. Only birdsong breaks the silence of this paradise on earth. The boys play in the waterways and look for frogs while Mary and I philosophise and reminisce about past lives and loves. It is dusk by the time we head for home, traversing the desert with a full moon anointing the magnificence of it all.

Khalifa is a sheik, and director of one of the Ruler's companies, and being a close friend of Mary's has offered to take the boys to watch him train his falcons in the desert. Falconry is an integral part of desert life, practised for centuries. Originally falcons were used for hunting, to supplement the Bedouin diet, but today falconry is sport.

Khalifa, wearing the traditional dishdasha, drives off road in his red four-wheel drive, with the boys bouncing up and down in the back while I cling to the armrest. We bump over dunes and down sandy tracks to a lower reach of desert on Dubai's fringe. The four-wheel drive following us contains his henchmen and a newly trained falcon, plus a cage of pigeons as live bait.

Khalifa straps a leather grip to his forearm, and his magnificent caged falcon is brought to him, released and placed onto his arm, the talons circling the armlet. A filigreed leather hood covers the falcon's head. One hundred metres away there is a shout as a pigeon is released from the cage. The hood is removed from the falcon's head and he flies with startling speed towards the pigeon, strikes it's neck in one deft bite, and the pigeon drops to the ground. The falcon then flies back to Khalifa to be rewarded with raw meat.

The boys stroke the falcon's breast feathers and Khalifa gently attaches leather arm protectors to their arms so they can

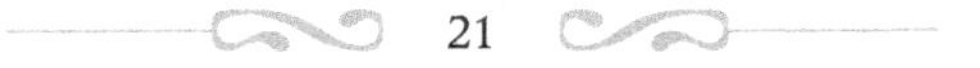

carry the falcon in turn, showing no fear at all, before we see a replay of the training session. Back home later, there is discussion about blood sports and cultural traditions, which ties me up in knots trying to seek the right answer for young and enquiring minds.

We spend days driving along *wadis*, (dry creek beds), where unexpectedly you might find spring water gushing into pristine pools, with frogs and water lilies, birds and butterflies, surprising us after driving through what seemed like barren and arid desert sands.

The Arabian Desert, it's awesome beauty, history and traditions, has cast its spell on me, and has supplied the boys with endless fodder for school projects. It will promote hours of discussion when we re-unite with the Disciple in Adelaide.

Postscript

Since 2013 it has been necessary to have a visa, ID or entry/exit forms to cross from UAE to the Buraimi Oasis.

Melodramas in Malawi (2010)

Don't think there are no crocodiles,
just because the water's calm

MALAWIAN PROVERB

We choose to explore Malawi, mainly because of the disciple's African childhood memories travelling to Nyasaland with his father, but also because I am keen to try birdwatching, centred on Lake Malawi. The lake covers one fifth of this landlocked country, and is its natural life-giving heart.

Malawi's ancient history was disturbed in the fourth century AD with the arrival of Bantu peoples, who introduced iron tools, and being ironworkers, set up kilns that lit the night skies. The Maravi Empire emerged (*maravi* meaning flames), which morphed into Malawi. Subsequently, trading posts were set up along Lake Malawi's shores, with Portuguese slave traders centering their activities here, before moving operations to coastal Mozambique.

In 1859, Scottish explorer David Livingstone discovered Lake Malawi, and gradually the British took control of the country, calling the region Nyasaland. They traded in tea and tobacco that filled colonial coffers for over 100 years. Malawi emerged independent in 1964.

With a bump and a screech of brakes, our flight from Johannesburg ends at Lilongwe, capital of Malawi, and after a

brief customs pantomime, we head for a light aircraft hangar. Here Charlie, a robust and hearty Malawian ex-fighter pilot, greets us and instructs us to climb aboard a small plane standing nearby. He jumps into the pilot's seat and starts the engine. It is a rather old-looking plane with its well-worn leather seats and frayed seat belts. 'She may look old, but her engine's brand spanking new,' says Charlie with a laugh. 'Buckle up, and we'll get this little baby moving,' he laughs.

I notice bulbous black clouds building in the distance, and a lightning fork spikes across the sky. I have no confidence whatsoever, but by this stage it is too late to contemplate flight conditions, we are careening down the runway, swooping over tropical greenery and taking off towards the storm. The lightning forks and black clouds are now left of the plane as we bank to the right. I begin to relax and Charlie, now we are airborne, is laughing and joking as a wonderland of lush forests and waterways spreads below us. Soon the vast expanse of Lake Malawi, more like an inland sea, glistens in the morning light.

The flight takes just thirty minutes, and we land on the private airstrip of Makakola Retreat, or 'Club Mak', as it is affectionately known by locals. This hotel lies on the southern shores of Lake Malawi, and we plan to spend time here, investigating the lake and hopefully finding my favourite bird species, the African fish eagle, to follow and watch.

Charlie lands his 'baby' with what you might call a flourish, and we bump our way along a dusty airstrip to a waiting jeep. Charlie cheerily waves us off, turns, and with a healthy rev of the engine, takes off into the blue. He will do a round robin of tourist flights over Malawi, returning at nightfall to Club Mak, where he and his plane are housed. At 6 am each day, the noisy

warm-up run of Charlie circling Club Mak is our alarm call for the day.

We soon blend with the relaxed tempo of Club Mak, living lakeside, watching water birds fossick in reed beds, and walking along garden pathways with heady aromas of jasmine and frangipani permeating our senses.

In the quest to find fish eagles, we meet Henry and Stanley, young Malawians, who will sail us to an island isolated in the lake's centre, and known for abundant birdlife. We plan to spend a day with binoculars and cameras, and take a hamper lunch generously packed by Violet, from Club Mak's kitchen. The catamaran, named *Club Mak 2*, lies on the bank and we set sail, clambering onto the central hull, which supports two pontoons, now slicing through the water as the wind fills the sails that clap noisily against a tall steel mast.

It is hot and steamy, and soon we are shedding clothes and layering zinc cream on faces and shoulders. Ebony-skinned Stanley chuckles and says, 'We don't need to do that!'

'Lucky you,' I reply. 'If we don't, we shall turn bright pink and suffer for a week with sunburn.'

Stanley and Henry are in their late teens, and were educated at a local school, streaming to a tourism accreditation, which gave them work at Club Mak. They are fluent in English, and have a wonderful and relaxed indifference to protocols, coupled with a deep pride in showing off their extraordinary country.

Sails are trimmed, and we are now speeding through the water with Henry's hand on the rudder as he maximises every wind gust, whilst barking the occasional order to Stanley. Soon we approach the island's protective cove and the boys drop anchor to the floor of an intimate bay, with rocks layering a

small beach. A buxom baobab tree prominently boasts its individuality against the tamarind and fig trees that shroud the island. The water is so clear that tiny pebbles reflect sparkles of light rippling on the surface, and small fish dart around like silver arrows. The silence is broken by the call of birds, and the gentle splash of water against the boat. We plump up beach towels and backpacks, propping ourselves in comfort against the mast to sit and watch.

We don't have long to wait before the distinctive caw of a fish eagle can be heard high above us in the baobab tree.

'Look, a nest,' says Stanley excitedly. 'It's a fish eagle!'

Through the leafy canopy we can see the nest, cleverly stabilised in a tree fork, with a magnificent fish eagle calmly perched, his talons circling a branch as he surveys the water below. The African fish eagle is known as the 'voice of Africa'.

They have two different calls, one is for 'in-flight' communication, the other a short 'quork' sound, which is the 'at home and on my perch' call. The plumage is dramatically beautiful with head, breast and tail feathers snowy white against a luxuriant brown feathered body and strong black wings spanning two metres. A featherless yellow head and cruel raptor's beak complete the picture of the rock star among the eagles of Africa.

Fish eagles practise pair fidelity, and it is likely that this fish eagle is calling out to his mate across the water. 'How do you know it's a male?' I ask, and Henry says the female is larger but he is only guessing. We hear an answering caw across the northern face of the island announcing the arrival of a huge eagle with a fish clasped within her talons. She swoops low over us, as if to show off her bounty, and ascends with a flap of wings to the nest, where there seems to be much excited eagle

conversation and excitement over the fish that is plonked into the nest and promptly devoured.

Later, both birds roost on a branch, nestling against each other like a feathered pyramid, their heads close together and in harmony after the hunt, the kill and the feast. As they sleep, we see hornbills preening themselves on lower branches. Weavers are busily weaving their nests, the male workaholic being bossed and bullied by the female weaver as to the design of the nest. If it is not up to scratch she will pull it apart, directing him to start again to meet her standards. There are herons at the water's edge, and splashes of vibrant blue as a kingfisher visits us. A white-throated long-tailed cormorant stalks his way around the rock pools in search of trapped fish for easy pickings.

Suddenly Henry alerts Stanley to a cloud build-up. Pitch-black clouds are moving across the horizon accompanied by lightning flashes and rumbles of thunder.

'We must head back instantly,' he says.

We bundle up clothing and hampers and the anchor is pulled up over the hull as Stanley pushes us off from an overhanging rock and jumps aboard. He starts an eggbeater engine – about as useful as an eggbeater, but we are in the calm before the storm and there is no wind to fill the sails. I realise the urgency involves lightning, and our very tall steel mast, which would be a perfect lightning conductor to fry us all with one strike. Both Henry and Stanley are white knuckled, matching the whites of their wide and terrified eyes as we endeavour to beat the storm across the lake, thunder claps and lightning flashes whipping the water behind us.

We at last drag *Club Mak 2* ashore and run indoors as torrential rain begins to fall. We congratulate the boys with a

generous tip for a job well done, then order medicinal and reviving gin and tonics.

A late morning walk winds us through lush tropical gardens and unbelievably we hear the strident sound of bagpipes playing 'Beyond Bonny Banks'! A wedding ceremony is taking place in a frangipani garden, with the bride being piped to the altar by two robust Scotsmen in full Scottish rig of kilts with black velvet jackets and lacy neck flounces. A beautiful Titian-haired bride in traditional white, but with a tartan sash, is being escorted by her father, also in a kilt, followed by a gaggle of child attendants.

'Scotland the brave!' I say. And brave indeed they are in this stifling humidity. The wedding guests wear light and more weather friendly clothing, but the Scottish influence is emphasised with a tartan scarf or bow tie.

Scottish culture is still a dominant part of Malawi. Blantyre, a major town, is named after Livingstone's birthplace in Scotland, and there have been 150 years of Scottish missions influencing and integrating with Malawian education.

We watch through a cover of bushland as vows are taken. Then the wedding party moves to a tartan-embellished marquee, where many a double malt is imbibed with each toast to the bride and groom, and lunch extends till nightfall, with Scottish reels and revelry.

The executive decision has been made to take a local bus to Blantyre, to connect with a flight out of Malawi. Hiring a taxi is not possible here, and Charlie's air charter service is unavailable. Mangochi, a nearby town, runs a mini-bus service to Blantyre, and we pile in with our luggage flung into a hatch at the back.

After sitting patiently for an hour I query the cause of the delay. I am told that the bus will only depart when full and there are two more empty seats. Finally a farmer with a sack of grain climbs in, squeezing the sack under his seat, and a small rip in the side sees a trickle of grain travel to the floor. His wife of no mean dimensions, arrives with a basket of produce from the markets, and settles herself next to the disciple, with a huge smile, and offers him a banana.

At last we move. This is definitely not express, we seem to stop every two miles to let people off, and take more on board. The driver, Friendly, is just that, and has witch doctor-type charms and dingle dangles hanging from his rear-vision mirror that jangle to his very loud African music, which he will not turn down. 'Not possible,' he tells me, 'just one volume.'

We are captured, and there is no other option but to stay on board and ride with this travelling circus to Blantyre. Two hours pass and the snail's pace of pick up and delivery continues with bursts of speed from Friendly, as he manoeuvres our bus, slams on the brakes and then overtakes people, carts, livestock and other buses along the way.

'If we survive this, we'll survive anything,' I say to the disciple, who is now eating a banana from the basket of produce next to him.

'Just relax and enjoy it,' he says.

We are items of extreme interest to local passengers, an unusual addition to their everyday travels. There is much laughter and a few questions to be answered, but above all a respectful kindness and concern for our comfort which, with legs akimbo to dodge luggage crammed around us, is an impossibility.

Three hours later we arrive in Blantyre accompanied by an afternoon storm of the same velocity as the day on the lake. The bus station is unsheltered, and drenched people huddle under colourful umbrellas, with the gutters gushing water that has nowhere to drain.

'Let's get a taxi to the hotel,' I say, and the disciple hails one with its window stuck open, a deluge of water teeming into the car as the driver laughs and shrugs his shoulders. Lightning forks crisscross the sky and a thunder clap threatens to propel us to the heavens.

Our final night in Malawi begins with strong gin and tonics, then delicious curries followed by tropical fruits. All windows and doors of the hotel are open to the elements to counter the heat and humidity, and so on retiring we also choose fresh air over a malfunctioning and smelly air conditioner in the bedroom. There are conical ceiling attachments holding mosquito nets that cascade over the beds, but as the disciple turns over to settle, he catches the net and the whole contraption falls from the ceiling on top of him. He spends his night with hands in prayer position over his nose to allow for breathing, the mosquito net covering him like a shroud.

The medicinal anti-malarial qualities of copious gin and tonics lull us to sleep, despite the constant whine of mozzies and the distant rumbles of thunder. Dawn finally breaks, bringing with it a deep reluctance to leave tantalising Malawi, with the temper tantrums of the wet season adding to our indelible memories!

Swedish Language School, Studies with Refugees (2011)

I will study and get ready,
and someday my chance will come

ABRAHAM LINCOLN

The trees are petrified in ice, with twigs and branches sparkling in the dawn light. It is 9 am and mid winter in Sweden, and I have spikes securely strapped to my boots to conquer ice patches along the walkway.

We are living in Alingsas, a country town nestled between two lakes and ringed by woodland yet only a forty-minute drive to Gothenburg. I am heading for the Utbildnings Hus (or Education House) as a new student of Swedish Language and Culture, which will entail four hours of class each day, and I shall be an oddity among the throngs of eager refugees who must take this course if they want to stay and work in Sweden.

Not being a refugee, it has taken months to plough through Swedish bureaucracy to achieve acceptance, but by using the strong case of having two little Aussie–Swede granddaughters, plus holding my Swedish residency status, any opposition is overruled and a tick is finally put beside my name.

The Utbildnings Hus is an imposing building by the river. As I approach I see veiled women wearing padded parkas with woollen scarves twirled around their veiled heads, and snow

boots peeping from voluminous skirts. Bicycles are stacked along the path into neatly slotted bike racks, and a group of leather-clad young men are smoking and laughing together as they lock up their bikes.

A beautiful face turns to me and smiles. '*Hej,*' she says in the Swedish greeting, 'I am Amina from Somalia.' I marvel at her perfect English and learn she has a degree in economics from London University, but has recently moved to Sweden in the hope of better job prospects and a more generous welfare system. Her story of seeking refuge began eight years ago when she escaped war-torn Mogadishu with nothing but a carpetbag of possessions.

Amina introduces me to Youi from Thailand, Maryam from Kabul, Fatima from Palestine, and Slavna from Serbia. There is no common language between us, so we communicate with smiles, laughter and dramatic gestures to tell of our marital status, children, siblings and the freezing Swedish weather.

I snap off the boot spikes and we enter a welcoming assembly hall, with admin on the left and a bistro area on the right. Here a United Nations of people are taking coffee together in small groups. Gudrun is manning the desk and my name is duly ticked. The classes are allotted according to education and background to allow students and teachers a better chance to progress as a group. Some of the refugees are virtually illiterate, and they will be gently and carefully nurtured in the Swedish system. Many in this category are elderly and some have recently migrated to Sweden to join their families already settled here. Their children are now literate, but they are not.

We walk past an auditorium with an amphitheatre layout and a dome-shaped glass roof consistent with a Swedish obsession

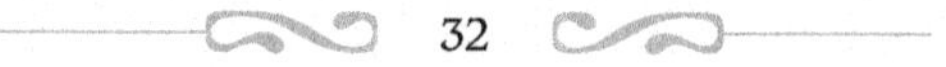

for natural light. When it is used for film screenings or theatre, an automated ceiling is activated to cover the glass dome.

Each classroom boasts a sea of computers, desks, chairs and whiteboards. I notice no shabby old furniture here and the room displays practical design and a clever use of space.

I am delighted to see Maryam and Amina are in my class, and Anki, who has been teaching Swedish here for many years, greets us. Tall and blond with clear blue eyes, she surveys her class and begins to speak. Every word spoken is Swedish, as we are tossed into the deep end. There are no translations, no explanations, just Swedish language ringing in our ears. The fifteen students in our class, all ages and stages, must stand, in turn, and following Anki's whiteboard directions, announce their name and country of birth in Swedish.

'Jag heter Heather, *och jag kommer fran Australien.'*

We have Afghanistan, Somalia, Lebanon, Iraq and Iran represented in our group, and after many repetitions, accents and voice ranges announcing names and birthplaces we emerge able to speak our first Swedish sentence with confidence.

We must only speak Swedish in the Utbildnings Hus, and will be smartly clipped into line by the teachers if we're not doing so. *'Bara Svenska! … bara Svenska!'*

In the bistro, we can revert to our mother tongues during a coffee break, before returning to class for two hours of headphones and slowly repeating Swedish after the prompt, all generated by computer. I am now speaking perfect Swedish, but don't understand a word of what I'm saying and fail to see the logic behind this method of teaching. I go home fighting back tears of frustration and the disciple cops a volley of verbiage about it all.

It is of course clever, as I find out over time, because by swamping our ears and senses in Swedish we slowly pick up speech patterns, phrases and words that will gradually integrate us into Swedish daily life. A computer program, individually pinned to each student, allows us to log on at home and progress at our own pace after the onslaught of the spoken word in class.

This pattern of student life continues, highlighted by watching Swedish films screened in the auditorium, visits to art galleries and museums, and slowly I have the confidence to speak more Swedish. I am surprised to find that my comprehension far exceeds my ability to speak.

Firm friendships are being made, and it is a privilege to hear firsthand stories of survival and harrowing escapes from tyranny and anarchy. Fatima and her family fled Palestine during the upheavals of the 1970s. They headed for Iraq and settled there, until the turmoil of Saddam Hussein's regime prompted them to pack up again and this time head for Sweden. Black-eyed and veiled, with face lines that map her extraordinary life, Fatima blesses Sweden every day.

'Here we have peace, no bombs! My children and grandchildren are safe, the schools are wonderful, and the Swedes are kind. We are happy!' she says to me in Swedish, as she speaks no English and I speak no Arabic.

Maryam is gentle, feminine and her shiny black hair is combed into a chignon under her veil. She and her family left Kabul with the impossibility of living under Taliban rule, being from the 'intelligentsia' in Afghanistan. 'Our beautiful country is ruined by hatred, suspicion and ignorance,' she says. She and her husband with two small children relax within the safe arms

of Sweden but pine and miss their country and those relatives still living there. 'This pain will never leave me,' she says.

I notice it is the women who seem to adapt with ease, but there are many problems hidden behind closed doors with their menfolk, who are now living in Sweden with its strong female culture; female equality in education and legal rights is mandatory here.

It is springtime and there is to be a wedding. Abdu and Abebi from Nigeria are students in our class and, being Christian, the Swedish congregation from the church in Alingsas has rallied around to decorate the church and conduct the service, and we are all invited to attend. The weather gods are smiling, providing blue skies and sunshine, and spring flowers line the pathway to the church door. Wafts of jasmine scent the air and birdsong competes with the gurgling stream winding along nearby.

The diversity of dress is glorious, with the brightest saris and silk scarves on show, brocaded dresses, and cabaret-style dressing mixing with the satin jackets, bow ties and hats for the men. I feel quite boring in my spring linen suit, but wear a flounce of jasmine on the lapel.

Abebi arrives, tall and ebony black with her glorious hair braided and dressed up. A tight white satin gown skims her figure, the skirt split to reveal white stilettos and a neat ankle. Abdu waits nervously with the pastor and his face breaks into a huge smile as she approaches him. The service is in Swedish and the church choir sings, and so do we, before spilling out into the sunshine. A buffet-style lunch has been laid out by the church women's group. It is a smorgasbord of seafood and salads, with creamy cakes to follow, and many and varied toasts to the bride and groom.

Slavna is from Serbia. Her background is Romany gipsy, one of the groups purged and suffering the genocide of the 1990s wars in the former Yugoslavia. She and her husband Goran fled to Sweden and are in the Swedish system but keen to speed the process. They work 24/7, doing any job possible (often for cash) to improve their lot. Slavna cleans schools and houses, irons clothes, and one day a week she cares for a disabled child. Goran is an outstanding tradesman and is never short of work. He feels the Swedish system is too slow and has used his ingenuity to improve their life. They are about to move into a bigger apartment.

It is now midsommar, the Swedish celebration that almost overrides Christmas. Midsommar, held over the summer solstice in June, begins with picking spring flowers and making wreaths, then adorning a maypole with flowers and greenery, and later singing and dancing around the maypole.

The Utbildnings Hus has organised a midsommar party in a nearby park, and the whole school community – teachers, students and their families, with all their children – will attend. Floral wreaths are placed on veiled heads and flowery boas circle men's necks. The music varies from Eastern to Western, and the dancing blends Africa and Asia with Europe. We have Arabs, Indians and Africans each interpreting their own version of how to celebrate the day.

The teachers move from group to group with platters of meatballs, cheeses, and sour fish to offer around; buffet tables are laden with salads and cakes. All races and cultures mix together, the curiosity and fascination between them encouraging a mingling, with much laughter and fun. The cultural mix continues when it is the children's turn to dance around the maypole.

This is a wonderful way to introduce Swedish traditions to refugees, allowing them to feel relaxed and part of this special day, and to understand a little more about their new homeland.

Learning Swedish at the Utbildnings Hus has been full of fun and laughter, despite language frustrations but, above all, it has lifted a veil to reveal the lives of courageous refugees, determined to make a better life in another culture.

Winter in Turkey (1989)

Stars are too far away for those with no plans to reach them

MEHMET MURAL IDAN

The fir trees carry a dusting of fresh snow and sunbeams play with the snow crystals that sparkle like fairy lights. The forest floor has a carpet of snow as soft as icing sugar and we imprint our boots through its virgin surface. At a clearing we see colourful kilims adorning benches and chairs around a lusty campfire, hand-held grills bearing lamb shashlicks and kebabs are sizzling and spitting, throwing out a tantalising smell of cooked meat and spice.

Around forty local Turks from Bursa have come to the mountain for a winter picnic, al fresco. The elders, shrouded by *kilims* and rugs, sit whilst the young cook and organise the feast. Children are building a snowman nearby, Turkish music vibrates from a ghetto-blaster, and the men are busy barbecuing and gossiping. Tables set up to the side bear platters of pita bread, olives and feta, roast potatoes and salads, super sweet deserts oozing syrup and Turkish delight.

We have been noticed and two young men beckon to us to join them, followed by a chorus of laughter and smiles of welcome from the others. We do look different, pallid and tall, with two small sons, one blond, the other a redhead – a stark contrast to the shorter, darker and more exotic looks of the Turkish party.

Shots of raki, the Turkish equivalent to ouzo, are offered to us, with soft drinks for the boys as we are introduced to everyone in their party, beginning with the elders. We speak no Turkish, and they have no English, but we find common ground in speaking German together.

'You are guests in our country, and we shall care for you', says Mehmet 'Please join us.' And, we happily do so.

This is an extended family feast day, and an easy thirty-kilometre escape from the bustling city of Bursa to the exquisite beauty of Uludag National Park. Uludag is the highest mountain in the Marmara region, which has passed from Roman, to Byzantine, and then to Ottoman rule. In ancient mythology, Uludag was the famed Mount Olympus, and they say the gods surveyed the Trojan War from this mountain.

The national park was a summer retreat for Romans to escape the heat of their capital city Bursa, and the ancient paved road they built can still be seen weaving its way to the mountain. The park is a wonderland of beech and fir trees, with diverse wildlife boasting twenty raptor species, including the golden eagle. At times there are still a few wolf packs to be heard howling to the moon.

Bursting with food, and dizzy with *raki*, we finally gather our boys and stagger our way back to the ski village, feeling more than 'cared for', as Mehmet promised. This has been yet another example of generous Turkish hospitality towards foreigners.

The decision to travel to Turkey for a ski holiday with the boys has been based on economics, the budget-priced family package is just possible for our stretched finances – and we have the bonus of a new and exotic country to discover.

We begin these series of adventures travelling by ferry from Yenikapi in Istanbul to Bursa, and then take the local bus service to Uludag. This bus has seen better days, and belches black smoke from its rear as it snails up the mountain, with a stop for the driver to secure snow chains onto the rear tyres. They cannot be too secure, because every revolution of the wheel, has a loose chain hitting the side of the bus. This does not concern the driver, who chain smokes his cigarettes and turns up the volume of Eastern music. Tassels, bells and evil-eye charms bounce and jangle around the windscreen.

The bus is filled with army personnel returning to their barracks near Uludag, and local women who've been shopping in Bursa. We are the focus of interest and everyone greets us. The boys are fed sweet treats, and red-haired Barney, to his horror, has his cheeks affectionately pinched by veiled matrons, who also ruffle his hair.

Uludag ski village is completely snowbound, and the bus slowly follows a snowplough clearing the road before us, spraying snow to each side as we enter the town square. We are staying at the Buyuk (Grand) Hotel, that overlooks ski runs and the waves of alpine peaks surrounding Uludag. We are the only foreigners here and are greeted by staff and other guests like celebrities, constantly being asked where we are from, and why we chose to ski in Turkey. Dinner in the Buyuk begins with guests assembling in a large lounge with open fireplaces, and ottomans placed around low tables where raki is served with appetisers of pistachios and crudités in fresh lemon juice.

I notice a group of important-looking Turks sitting by the lounge entrance, and as each guest enters they bow to them, a formal greeting. We learn it is the owner of the hotel and

his family, and they are observing protocols by personally welcoming guests to dinner. Waiters discreetly approach each group announcing that dinner is served, and we go to the dining room where gentle music, still Turkish but minus the deafening decibels, is being played by a small band. Candles are lit and guests sit in family groups.

It is wise to realise there will be six courses, and not to remark on the delectable food in order to avoid an immediate second helping. There is a look of sad astonishment if you decline a course. Turkish coffee in Ottoman-styled pots is served with Turkish delight, bulging with soft walnuts and powdered in icing sugar.

The dance floor fills with young and old, twirling and swirling to the Eastern music. Finally we join in, not knowing quite what to do, but the infectious fun around us dispels any inhibitions we might have had. We twist and sway with the other guests, who gradually peel off to the games rooms for cards and backgammon.

A clear sunny day dawns, and with skis clipped on we investigate the ski lift system. We find that each slope seems to have a different owner requiring multiple ski tickets. Being competent skiers we had hoped to ski all the runs of Uludag.

'This will cost us a fortune,' I say to the disciple, and ask to speak with the manager to discuss the problem. Soon, the important-looking Turkish gentleman from last night's dinner approaches us, bows, and with perfect English asks us our names and welcomes us to Uludag.

'My name is Bulent,' he says, 'and I own the Buyuk Hotel and the main ski lift runs.

The other slopes are not as long or as interesting, and I

would be honoured if you use my lifts for your holiday, as a token of my surprise that an Australian family has chosen to ski here in Turkey.' He then invites us to join his family for lunch at the mid-station restaurant, set in a small dip, on his ski terrain. The restaurant features a sun-soaked terrace for dining and people watching.

Bulent Bey (Bey is a mark of respect, used after a Turkish forename) is in his late sixties, with thick white hair, dark bushy brows that rim twinkly brown eyes, and laughter lines that extend to his cheeks. He has a courtly attention to manners and formality, and he listens but then quietly directs conversation from family, to Turkey's place in the world, and then exclaims: 'Why does Europe ignore us!' – then it's back to family matters again.

I discover he has married three times, and has a daughter and a recently married son. And there are others, plus grand-children, all a bit hard to quantify, but it is obvious who runs the show. There is a warmth and friendliness extended to us with great interest in our boys from younger members of the family, who, to my astonishment, remark on their good manners.

The boys are keen to ski, and I suspect to show off their skills to Bulent Bey, which they do to great effect. Bulent declares: 'We have two young Australian ski racers here in Uludag.'

There is a dress circle of chairs and tables set out in the snow at the bottom of the ski runs, where people can watch skiers while lazing in the sun, and perhaps drinking piping hot *salep*, a delectable white and creamy Turkish concoction. Here we see the well-heeled of Istanbul, wearing furs and exotic ski wear but preferring to be spectators, not skiers, as they socialise and promenade at the base of the slopes.

Bulent has now adopted us, and when his Istanbul family return home he seeks our company every day, either by inviting us for lunch in his small chalet, or joining us for dinner at the hotel followed by backgammon or cards – which he inevitably wins. He is a modern version of a feudal lord. All staff at the hotel, his chalet, restaurants, and ski lifts are locals, and under his supervision and care. He knows every family, most of whom live in villages adjacent to Uludag, and it is obvious to see the affection and respect he commands is genuine. One night he is visiting a workman's sick wife in hospital, the next he is organising education for a bright young village boy.

We are privileged to be in his entourage. The village recognises us now, as Bulent Bey's Australian friends. Arriving for dinner at his chalet we are greeted by Aydin, Bulent's housekeeper and chef. He takes our coats and directs us to the cozy lounge room, where Bulent waves us a greeting but is focused on a phone call.

The heavy snow of the past week, followed by the sunny warmth of today, has triggered an avalanche, which has covered an area near houses on his estate.

He immediately actions all staff, snowploughs and tractors to go and help, with emergency services alerted in Bursa. His chalet is the nerve centre of operations, and we watch in admiration before he summons his driver Erdem to take him to the site to oversee the disaster. The next morning we hear that mercifully no lives were lost, and there has been minimal damage to property.

We are now armed with some Turkish, and can at least greet, thank, and order food without too much trouble. This effort delights locals, who are treating us as if we are locals too.

After a farewell lunch and a final ski, it is: '*Gule, gule!*' to Bulent Bey and Uludag and a promise to return as we board the bus for Bursa.

Cekirge is a suburb of Bursa, lying at the foot of Uludag where thermal springs of 40°C, gush to the surface of the hillside. These healing waters have been used for centuries as health cures, and are trapped into baths and spas usually built in marble. Hotels built on top of the thermals surround the majestic Mosque of Murat.

Our little hotel, with backpacker rates, is in a back street behind the mosque. Our small room has four bunk beds and an open window framing the mosque's minarets. It's basic accommodation, but clean. Three generations of family run the hotel, with Grandma in the kitchen, and Mama at reception. We walk down three flights of stone steps to a basement of marble-sculptured lion heads, mouths wide open, spraying steaming water into marble baths built for two. The excess water overflows into cisterns and drains to who knows where.

Aching ski legs and muscle maladies are instantly salved after we immerse ourselves into waters rich with sulphur, sodium, calcium, and magnesium – a wonderful balm from our planet's heart. The soporific effect of the spa is instant, and the hard little bunks have no chance of delaying sleep, until 6 am, when our window facing the minarets almost shatters with the megaphone vibrations as a resounding 'call to prayer' is yelled from the mosque.

We decide another visit to the basement spa is the only remedy and, later, after warm pita bread with olives and feta and reviving Turkish coffee, we are ready to head for Pamukkale and Istanbul.

But, that is another story!

Riding Istanbul's Magic Carpet (1989)

If earth were a single state,
Istanbul would be its Capital

NAPOLEON BONAPARTE

With due respect to Napoleon Bonaparte, I have traversed more of this world then he, and I totally agree with his assessment of Istanbul. The ethereal minarets of Santa Sophia, the sprawling opulence of Topkapi Palace, the bustling Bosphorus, with its ships and ferries, bridges and fishing boats, make Istanbul feel like the epi-centre of civilisation.

We are huddled together from the chilly winds of January beside the Bosphorus, waiting for fresh fish to be cooked on a brazier set up at the back of a fishing boat.

Fish are hooked, flicked off the line, gutted and flipped onto a pan to sizzle before being sandwiched into fresh rolls, with a squeeze of lemon juice, and then passed across to us on the wharf.

This delicious snack is taken as we walk to the Egyptian Bazaar, and soon the smell of spices and *salep* wafts out of a grand old building, the centre of spice trade in Istanbul for centuries past. It was built in 1660 AD by the Ottomans as a bazaar exclusively for trade in spices, but today Turkish confectionary and stalls selling perfume oils have broadened its base. As we enter the arched colonnades, we see tiers of Turkish

delight lining the shop fronts and sample trays enticing you to try before you buy.

I try pistachio and coconut, with almonds sunk into the rose-flavoured sweet. The nuts are soft and succulent, permeated with a flavour of roses, and if the gods serve sweets in Paradise, this could be their choice as a heavenly treat. The disciple and our sugar-primed sons work the sample trays from stall to stall as I investigate the spices displayed in hessian sacks. Vendors scoop spice onto scales, then fill paper bags with a flourish to the queue of waiting buyers, all local Turks.

Being winter and armed with a few words of Turkish, we feel less like tourists and more like locals, even though we do look different. Our attempts to order are greeted with delight and generosity. Small alcoves have tables and stools crammed together where sweet black tea is served. Another alcove has a clutch of Turkish old boys sitting on ottomans, smoking hubble-bubble pipes together, philosophising, or perhaps discussing politics.

Turkish music can be heard as a background to the bustle of commerce in the main arcades, but with the boys feeling rather sick after so much Turkish delight, we decide to walk to the Grand Bazaar, and thankfully the freezing temperatures outside dispel their nausea along the way. The Grand Bazaar was first constructed in 1455 AD, after the Ottoman conquest, and began as a covered bazaar devoted to textiles. Steady expansion added porticoed malls housing antiquities, carpets and kilims, gold and silver, with an old books market built beside the Beyazid Mosque. By the seventeenth century, the Grand Bazaar was central to all Mediterranean trade, and comprised 3000 shops, five mosques, seven fountains, and eighteen gates. The gates were shut at night, to mark the end of the day's trade.

Today the noise and bustle of commerce is little changed, with manners and formality screening native cunning to achieve sales. We are ushered into a carpet store, where rugs and ottomans line the floor and kilims (rustic and brightly coloured hand-woven rugs) are folded and stacked to the ceiling. On being seated, a young boy enters with a tray of steaming apple tea, served in small glasses, each sitting on a silver saucer. The tea is sweet and delicious, and now settled we are at the mercy of the vendor, who scatters five kilims across the floor for us to admire, admire the patterns and study the textures.

He mentions prices which, we have been warned, start at three times the real value. 'My best price for the first sale of the day,' he tells us. The drama of bargaining is all part of the fun, and when we finally agree on a rug and a price, his look of sad resignation is accompanied by: 'How can I survive, when I sell at these low prices!' masking a glint in his eyes, as he gently wraps the kilim in brown paper and ties it with string. We pay in US dollars, which will give him an added bonus on the robust black market in currencies.

The Grand Bazaar is a city within a city. Each day there are new arcades to explore, with each section devoted to similar merchandise: porcelain, with pots, urns and tiles painted by hand and featuring the deep Izmir blue and burnished orange colours of traditional Ottoman designs; hand-woven carpets in a central square, where bespoke silk carpets may cost over $100,000 and can be seen in Middle Eastern palaces and mosques; junk shop arcades featuring ancient coffee pots and lamps that promise Aladdin; a leather precinct and a gold souk with jewellery and ancient gold coins command another maze of alleyways; the textile stores, featuring silks, brocades and

embroidery from central Asia, have kept alive the Silk Road caravan; and the antique books market is a feast for history scholars, with ancient handpainted parchments and exquisite calligraphy from Persia depicting marauding tribes waving their scimitars as they gallop to victory.

The boys buy wooden pencil cases, inlaid with mother-of-pearl images of horsemen and scimitars. I am weighed down with Izmir-blue porcelain pots and a horrified husband, wondering how on earth they will travel home to Australia.

I decide to indulge in the therapy and warmth of Istanbul's famous Turkish bath, the Cemberlitas Hamam, built in 1584 AD. A small doorway leads to an reception area with a central lounge for tea and refreshments, where men and women may mix after the segregated bathing rituals. Armed with towels and a locker key, I am lead to the female hamam, and wearing a towel and bath slippers enter the bath chamber. A circular marble platform (*sicaklik*) is centred under an enormous dome with glass skylights, allowing sunbeams to play with exquisitely honed marble alcoves and sculptured gargoyles, spilling hot thermal water into small pools.

There are dozens of naked women of all ages, talking and laughing as they are scrubbed and douched with bowls of steaming water, or standing under gargoyles of gushing water from Mother Earth's heart. Often three generations of family will meet at the hamam to relax together, gossip and enjoy this ancient Turkish ritual.

I watch a grandmother pouring water over her young granddaughter, who squeals with delight.

I lie prone on the marble *sicaklik* heated by thermals to be scrubbed pink by a genial and robust bath attendant, whose ample bosom bounces and 'tuck shop' arms shudder as she energetically scrubs my whole being. She then thoroughly sluices me with buckets of water, and directs me to the marble spa pool to immerse and relax. Never have I felt so cleansed! An hour is then spent in a bathrobe, reclining on a lounge bed and sipping hot apple tea.

The disciple and boys have been combing the Grand Bazaar for *kehribar* (the Turkish word for amber) without success. Amber is fossilised tree resin, and often insects are captured inside. The resin slowly hardens over time, becoming a transparent golden clump. It is then fashioned and polished into jewellery and ornaments. They have been told that Kadikoy, on the Asian side of Istanbul, is a possible source.

Istanbul is split by the Bosphorus. The Anatolian or Asian side meeting the Sea of Marmara is rarely visited by tourists, who focus more on Istanbul's city centre, lying to the west of the Bosphorus. Ferries crisscross these waterways from the Black Sea to the Sea of Marmara, so we board a ferry to the Asian side to wander around Karikoy's famous marketplace in search of amber. On board, we meet a friendly Australian couple (I would say in the 'grey nomad' category), who have taken the ferry to see Istanbul landmarks from the water.

This is their first trip overseas, and having just arrived in Turkey they are a little hesitant as to directions. After our two-month odyssey of Turkey I feel qualified to advise, so I confidently direct them to get off at the next port for an easy walk to their hotel in Taksim. We wave them a fond farewell as they disembark, and watch them disappear into the crowd of people at the wharf. The ferry continues and, to my horror, I realise I've sent them to a port on the Asian side of Istanbul,

where literally no one speaks English, where all the signs are in Turkish, and from where it would take them all day to walk to Taksim! I still blush with shame, when I think about this incident.

We buy unhoned amber in a Karikoy bazaar, and discover that Anatolian Istanbul is emphatically Asian, with a vibrancy and ambience possibly unchanged since the glorious days of Constantinople. The ferry ride back to Eminonu is rough, with biting winds gusting off the Bosphorus, so we decide to take a taxi to our little hotel. The traffic is in gridlock and our driver speaks no English, so we all try to communicate, chiming in with monosyllables and using sign language. A car full of Turks adjacent to us watch with amusement. A friendly face leans out of the window and asks: 'Do you want some help?' With that, he gets out of the car and climbs into our taxi, squeezing next to us in the back seat. He then interprets the destination to our driver, and with us all laughing and cheering, returns to his car full of friends and they shout: *'Gule gule!'* to us, just as the traffic starts to move again. Our driver manages a hair-raising manoeuvre to change direction and we head for home.

Australia's Turkish links were cemented by Gallipoli, and endorsed by the immortal words of Kemal Attaturk: 'Your sons, having lost their lives on this land, are now our sons as well.' This magic carpet ride through Istanbul has shown us that Attaturk's extraordinary generosity of spirit is alive and well in Turkey today.

Outback South Australia (2014)

The Outback is four-fifths of the continent, and it's at the heart of our ethos

JACK THOMPSON

With all our family now living in Europe, I am trying to keep alive six generations of Australian heritage. Whistle-stop visits to Adelaide are just that, so I lock in a three-day outback adventure to coincide with Toby's business trip to Adelaide in May.

The three of us board a Qantas Link prop-jet bound for Roxby Downs, along with tattooed miners, sultry teenagers in frayed denim, a colourfully dressed Indian family. We climb the ladder gangway to enter a small cabin that gives each seat a window.

Thirty years ago, Roxby Downs was a cattle station, and when the mining town was built on this site the name was retained. Roxby Downs has since serviced one of the world's largest mines, yielding copper, uranium and gold.

The flight takes ninety minutes and the noise of the prop. jets prevent easy conversation, but as the sheer enormity of the landscape unfolds, with colours changing from mellow beige to golds, then to russet red, everyone is glued to their windows.

Roxby airport is out of town, and with no transfer booked we accept a ride with Todd, a local miner, who tosses our backpacks into his ute tray. We squeeze in next to him, with

Toby opting for the dickie seat behind, which he shares with a chainsaw and a jerry can of diesel. Todd has just celebrated his mother's sixtieth birthday in Adelaide: 'Geez, I last three days in that place,' he says. 'Cities aren't for me, too many people. You can breathe out here in the bush!' And it's clear he's happy to be home as he drops us off at the Oasis Motel in downtown Roxby and with a cheery wave roars off to meet his mates at the pub.

The Roxby Downs pit stop allows us to link with Wrightsair, a scenic flights business based at William Creek, the perfect hub for exploring Lake Eyre, the Painted Hills of Anna Creek, and Coober Pedy. There is no need to set alarms in Roxby, the screeching corellas ensure we're awake at dawn and well able to meet the deadline of an early departure with Wrightsair.

Troy, the pilot, is moving the propeller backwards and forwards and checking wing flaps when we arrive. The plane is tiny, and we squeeze our backpacks into the tail hold and climb aboard. Troy is immaculately rigged in bush gear and aviator sunglasses, and greets us with a wry smile. 'Who wants to be co-pilot?' he asks. I'm selected, with the disciple preferring not to watch the cockpit instruments spin around, and Toby planning to photograph Olympic Dam from the lower windows in the back seat. We buckle up and I have an earphone connection to air traffic control, plus a joystick, disturbingly close by, as Troy twiddles dials and presses buttons before starting the engine. There is an instant response, and the propeller swings to life and sends a shudder through the cabin.

Soon we are soaring over the red gibber towards Olympic Dam, a gigantic hole gouged into the earth's crust with tiered roadways around its rim where trucks can be seen shunting ore

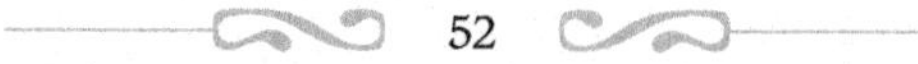

to a railway siding. In the distance, Lake Eyre emerges as a sea of salt, so glaringly white you need very dark shades to cope with the view.

In 1964, Donald Campbell achieved the land speed record of 649 km per hour here, and opened the world's eyes to the spectacle of Lake Eyre. Further back in history, the lake claimed many of our colonial fathers, with islands on the lake named after explorers who did not survive. Today, when Queensland receives heavy monsoonal rain, the river systems will eventually spill into the lake, which instantly erupts with bird migrations, fish and flora. Today it is dry, the water evaporated or sunk into the saltpan.

Just one month ago, a recreational pilot (the word 'recreational' is emphasised by Troy) landed his ultralight plane on the lake, and promptly got stuck in the salt. Stranded passengers had to be rescued by helicopter. 'This takes outstanding pilot skill,' says Troy, 'because the sea of salt distorts any sense of height.' The stricken plane eventually sank through the salty crust to be preserved for eternity, another misadventure to add to the lake's folklore.

William Creek's runway cuts a line in the sand beside Australia's smallest town, boasting two motels, a pub, a camping ground, and the only petrol station to be found between Maree and Coober Pedy. William Creek lies on the Tirari Desert, where sand dunes with corridors of gibber and open scrublands are crisscrossed with water courses and flood plains. After rain, the dunes are carpeted with wild flowers, and there are intermittent waterholes to sustain red gums and coolibah trees. It is a popular staging post for 'grey nomads' in their camper vans, and international backpackers.

We land with a bump and notice a tractor the size of a quad bike towing a light aircraft into a hangar. It looks like *Noddy in Toytown.* Trevor Wright, of Wrightsair, is driving the tractor and he manages the William Creek pub as well. He detaches the tractor from the Cessna and drives over to greet us, shouting above the noise of the tractor: 'Welcome to William Creek! Just walk up to the pub and they will settle you in!' So, with backpacks and fly nets in place, we walk a good mile to the pub as Troy flies over us, en route to his next pick-up in Coober Pedy. There is a 'do it yourself' expectation in the outback, breeding self-reliant individuals, well able to survive the extremes of life here. Modern conveniences are mostly shunned, as a soft way out of life's reality.

We enter the pub through Dingo's Bar, where the owner's tame dingo likes to sleep on a cushion, and a large picture of him hangs over the door. Inside is the main bar, where thousands of pictures, international emblems, flags, and signatures of famous people are plastered all over the walls and ceiling. Stools line the bar, but basically it is a stand-up facility, and a popular retreat for jackaroos from nearby Anna Creek cattle station.

Recently this pub featured in the film *Last Cab to Darwin* starring Michael Caton, and we can see why. It is fun, and you are welcomed and accepted as a 'bushie' from the back of beyond, even if you're city slickers, like us. We register with Juliette, on a working holiday from France, and with a delicious accent and friendliness she directs us to the accommodation in a small wing of motel type units at the back of the pub.

A blood-red sunset lights up the gibber, with streaks of red turning cloud wisps to mauve, and dead tree skeletons around the pub are dotted with white corellas, now silent, as evening

calms their raucous arguments. A hum of activity and laughter comes from the pub, where campers, jackeroos and locals have gathered, so we head for the bar. Holding court is Tim, the truckie, resplendent in a high-viz vest, with tattooed forearms that he waves expressively to emphasise each yarn.

Tim is of robust build, and peppers his stories with outback Aussie slang, sitting on a bar stool and surrounded by listeners. He delivers gas and fuel to the outback, with his run including Anna Creek station and Coober Pedy. He's just driven eleven hours from Adelaide, and he will pit stop here for the night.

An Italian family from Milan add another dimension to the gathering, and a honeymoon couple from England's landed gentry (he is a Lord) share a champagne tete-a-tete. Jackaroos, glowing with the healthy outdoor life and extremes of nature that Anna Creek provides, add an electric element to the group, which strikes a chord with our euro-centric son, who is somewhat tinged with envy.

Dinner is served on long tables with bench seating, and we join Tim and order Anna Creek rump steaks as we hear more of his sagas and bush yarns involving snakes, blow outs, and flash floods. He retires early, with another twelve-hour day ahead and no doubt more adventures. The night sky displays the Milky Way in all its glory, unpolluted by city lights, and it is so clear you feel within arm's length of the stars, with a full moon casting ghostly shadows across the scrubland.

The shrieking corella alarm call ensures we wake in time for our flight to Coober Pedy. This time we are driven to the airstrip by the beautiful Camille, who will pilot the four-seater Cessna. We wear headphones to bar engine noise, allowing us to talk with her during the flight.

We take off over Anna Creek station, which at 24,000 square kilometres is about the size of Holland, and head for the Painted Hills, which can only be seen by air. This lunar landscape of ochre mounds has evolved over millions of years, with water from floodplains and rivers oxidising the manganese and iron into vivid reds, yellows and stark white, covering twenty kilometres by ten kilometres. We swoop down to 500 feet, and see chasms of ochre and white in linear form, but curving along the mounds, rather like the brush strokes of a child's first painting. 'I never get tired of seeing them,' says Camille. 'You discover a new shape or pattern every time you fly here.'

Coober Pedy promises excitement. We land before a heat mirage that hovers over the runway's end. The name originated as the Aboriginal 'Kupa-piti', meaning 'White man's hole', and since 1915 Coober Pedy has been the world's major source of gem-quality opals. Hillocks of mines puncture the landscape as we head for town, and below ground there are houses, churches, and art galleries. They are known as 'dug outs', and enjoy stable temperatures between 23 and 25°C all year, ensuring an escape from the scorching heat above ground.

Vlad migrated from Czechoslovakia to Australia, joining bands of Yugoslavs, Greeks, and Poles who descended on Coober Pedy in the 1960s, lured by the prospect of riches, coupled with a desire to escape political oppression at home.

For decades he has mined and marketed opals. He has experienced the mercurial fortunes of all prospectors but still has the will to continue and find that unsurpassable vein of black opal. We spend the day with him, touring mines and viewing his prize stones for sale.

The opal's history is long and enmeshed in superstition. In

the Middle Ages, opals were talismans for good luck, as their spectrum of rainbow colours represented every gem, in just one stone. After Sir Walter Scott's novel was published, involving holy water, an opal, and the heroine's death, opals became symbols of bad luck (demonstrating the power of popular writers in 1829). In 2015 the market for opals is huge, and an exhibition at the Adelaide Museum showcases one exquisite white opal, worth $1 million.

Sleeping underground in Coober Pedy gives the indescribable feeling of being cocooned within Mother Earth, and I muse at the attraction of being a Hobbit.

These past few days glimpsing outback life, its people and customs, has re-grounded generational links to outback South Australia, with Toby determined to bring his little Swedes here soon to do the same.

Brindisi by Train (1983)

It's not an adventure unless there's a tinge of danger,
but life's greatest danger is not choosing adventure

BRIAN BLESSED

Milano Centrale, built with opulent extravagance in 1931, is the main railway station of Milan and boasts a seventy-two-metre vaulted ceiling and twenty-four platforms that branch from arched walkways.

It is 11 pm, and after a 'slo-mo' train trip from Austria I must change trains in Milan to continue south to Brindisi, where there's a ferry connection to Greece. I'm wearing a fur-trimmed suede coat and matching fedora, complete with a plume of feathers, à la Austrian countess, and I pull on gloves to fend off the bitter cold.

The box containing a noisy cuckoo clock, that 'cuckoos' every time it is bumped, is looped under one arm, whilst the free arm carries a case crammed with tourist treasures and clothing. These are the days before wheelie suitcases, and before I learnt to carry less luggage.

All information booths are closed, and even cafes have shut their doors. The atmosphere is unfriendly and aggressive, with the main hall dimly lit. It seems that many here are taking trips of a different kind, huddled into dark alcoves and behind huge pillars, with the sweet smell of non-nicotine smoke wafting through the night air, and the exchange of packets for money with the occasional altercation.

There is a complete absence of police and railway guards seem to be on board the trains sheltering from the cold. So, being alone, and looking 'faux' well-heeled, I suddenly feel vulnerable. And then I notice two skinny and swarthy youths, who are walking close beside me. I stop, and stare them down summoning an imperious demeanour and say, '*Va via, vattene!*' They respond to my Italian order to go away, perhaps they will try for more accessible prey. I spot a small group of Americans talking loudly together, and plonk my luggage near them. The cuckoo clock emits a series of cuckoos.

Mercifully there is a timetable on the wall. The overnight train to Brindisi will depart at midnight, from this platform, so I excuse myself to the Americans, and ask if I might wait with them until my train departs. 'Sure thing, little lady,' is the reply, in a deep southern drawl, and I forgive the 'little lady' in sheer relief to be part of a group as I wait. Their train for Venice leaves at 12.30 am, and so I am escorted to the Brindisi train, with my sleeping compartment found, before they bid me farewell and return to the platform.

The sleeper carriage is packed. I am sharing a compartment with an Italian couple travelling to San Marino, on the Adriatic coast. We manage to communicate with single words, hand gestures, and facial expressions, and they become very concerned when I tell them my destination is Brindisi.

'*Stare attento, stare attento*!' says Luigi, warning me to be careful.

Maria points to my rings and directs me to swivel the stones to face my palm. '*Brindisi molti problemi!*' she says emphatically.

I notice that Luigi is double locking our compartment door, and we pull the convertible seats into flat beds and prepare to sleep. I am instructed to sleep in the central bed, with Luigi facing the compartment door, as protector and guard for the night. Maria is by the window. We are sandwiched head to toe along our beds quite comfortably. Blankets are unfolded from top lockers, and pillows with clean white cases are distributed as the train clickety clacks into motion, moving out of Milano Centrale.

Disturbing train robberies, mainly in Eastern Europe, have been happening recently. Crime gangs have gassed compartments or even a whole carriage, to allow them free access to all baggage and valuables while the passengers are passed out. So Luigi's attention to our door lock, and his insistence on having freezing air coming in from an angled window vent, makes sense.

The overnight train to Brindisi is not express, and just before arriving at Bologna, there is a loud knocking at our door and: '*Controllo passaporti!*' Luigi tentatively opens the door to reveal two customs officers peering inside. Our passports are checked and documented, and I get the distinct feeling that these officials are peppering their night shift with the joy of disturbing the slumbers they would prefer to be having themselves.

I am in a twilight zone of dreams and nightmares, as the train speeds for a time, and then slows down to mark the next stop of the journey. We are now tracing the Adriatic coast from Rimini, according to the loudspeaker blaring its name. The next stop is San Marino, where the delightful Luigi and Maria gather their belongings and provide more directions for me to be careful and an '*arriverderci!*'. They depart, leaving me with a four-hour solo journey to Brindisi.

It is now 7 am, and a watery sunrise with misty blues and pinks light the sky over the Adriatic. I have an hour before arrival and my thoughts of a strong coffee and sweet biscotti motivate a walk through the carriages, only for me to find the restaurant car was uncoupled in Rimini.

Suddenly we stop. There is no station in sight, just farm orchards and pleasant countryside. An hour passes with no progress, so I wander through the carriage trying to find someone who speaks English. I notice no one seems to be agitated by the delay, so I keep knocking at each compartment door with: '*Parla inglese?*'

Finally the answer is 'yes!' and I'm invited to sit with Marco a student, and three older men, travelling on business to Brindisi. The guard has just informed them that, due to industrial problems at the Brindisi Petrochemical Plant, workers have detonated Molotov cocktails on all railway lines entering the town to draw attention to their safety concerns and pay conditions.

Antonio offers a bottle of homemade limoncello, a delectable lemon liqueur, and we hand round the bottle taking shots out of the lid, which on an empty stomach is swirl-making – but welcome.

Marco's father is a porter at Brindisi station, and has been in contact through the train's communication system. Marco offers me a lift to Brindisi; his father will drive here to pick us up. Other passengers are making urgent arrangements with taxi companies, and Italian rail is sending buses to collect stranded passengers who have less money, and more time on their hands.

We get off the train and walk through an orchard to the roadside. The sun is warm and the birds are singing as we find a fence to prop against, under a shady tree. Marco is studying

engineering in Florence, and is on his way home for a holiday break to catch up with family. I remark on his excellent English, and he says, 'In Italy, English is now second language if you want to be educated and to progress in a career.'

A white Fiat Cinquecento is speeding towards us. An arm waves through the sunroof and with a slam of brakes stops beside us. Roberto jumps out and with a bow takes my hand to welcome and apologise for the train incident. My large case is put in the boot with the hatch left open, so it just fits. Marco sits in the back with his backpack on his knees, and I sit in front, clutching the cuckoo clock, with the fedora firmly planted on my head and the feather plume blowing through the sunroof opening as we set off.

Roberto does not have much English, and fires Italian at Marco, who translates for me. He is saying that Roberto and Bella are inviting me to spend time at their home until the Brindisi ferry departs tonight at 10 pm, and would I accept and be their guest for the day. I do so with '*molto grazie*' while Roberto, determined to show off his driving skills, is weaving through traffic. We wind around Brindisi's streets, with every bump marked by a loud 'cuckoo!' We finally pull up at an apartment block, not far from the port.

Bella is at the door to greet us. She hugs her son with screams of delight, and then welcomes me to their home. The apartment is on the third floor, and after climbing the stairs we enter a comfortable entrance hall strewn with rugs, mirrors reflecting pictures of ships, a crucifix and the Madonna hanging over a sideboard. I am lead to Roberto and Bella's bedroom, where I am told to sleep for a few hours to recover from the train journey – on fresh linen that has been changed especially for their visitor.

Sleep comes easily, possibly helped by the limoncello, and it's about 2 pm when I'm awoken by a gentle tap on the door to join the family for lunch. The terrace overlooks the port of Brindisi, and a long table is laden with proscuitto, cheeses and breads, olives and fruit, with a tureen of steaming minestrone in the centre.

Marco and sisters Consuela and Adriana join Roberto and Bella, and I am plied with questions about Australia, and life there, with much fun and laughter discussing kangaroos and sharks. After lunch, Marco suggests we four wander the streets of Brindisi to see the sights; his parents will stay home, but later take me to the ferry.

Brindisi was a Greek stronghold before the Roman Empire took control, and the name means 'deer's head', referring to the natural shape of the harbour. Famous for its Roman heritage, Brindisi marks the end of the Appian Way from Rome, the paved 'foot-slog' for legions of soldiers. It was also known as the 'Gateway to the East', and was a main port for the merchants of Venice. The twelfth-century Duomo (cathedral) was destroyed by an earthquake in 1743, and all that remains is exquisite mosaic flooring, over which the new cathedral was built.

My delightful teenage guides are not only fluent in English, but have a detailed knowledge and pride in their home town. We walk to see these wonders and although it's now late afternoon, the sun is warm and the light dappled, with mellow hues accentuating the beauty and elegance of ancient times.

We return home to a farewell prosecco with Roberto and Bella, and later exchange addresses. My hope is that I can one day return their hospitality. The trusty Fiat Cinqucento is loaded with my luggage, with the cuckoo clock resting in the

dicky seat as Roberto drives to the port. He escorts me up the ferry's gangway before instructing the waiting purser to take care of this Australian lady.

I stand by the railings to wave him goodbye, now feeling part of his family. The dire warnings of '*Stare attento a Brindisi*' have been turned on their head, replaced with words like kindness, care, happiness and family unity.

In the Arabian desert with Khalifa and the falcons he trains.

The Buraimi Oasis bordering the UAE and Oman.

Desert elephants in Kunene region of Namibia.

The shores of Lake Malawi.

Bulent Bey and the disciple chewing the fat in Uludag, near Bursa, Turkey.

Admiring the spices at the Egyptian Bazaar spice markets in Istanbul.

Feeding wild hyenas at the city wall of Harar, Ethiopia.

The hyenas of Harar waiting to be fed.

Local fishermen in Dar es Salaam.

Exploring water springs near Muscat.

An elder counting his takings at the Muttrah Souk in Oman.

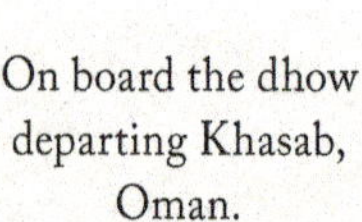

On board the dhow departing Khasab, Oman.

Dhow drifting the Musandam fjords in Oman.

A mother and son wrestle before boarding the bus for Konya in Turkey.

How to sell lottery tickets – Konya, Turkey.

Barney immersed in the 35°C hot springs of Pamukkale.

The thermal pools of Pamukkale.

Ethiopia – Harar and Hyenas (2008)

The hyena of your own country
does not break your bones

GIRYAMA PROVERB

The walled city of Harar in eastern Ethiopia beckons as a different adventure, being an Islamic pocket within Christian Orthodox Ethiopia – with the added incentive of feeding hyenas by the city wall at dusk. We decide to investigate.

The 500-kilometre road from Addis Ababa to Harar is a mire of untended potholes, especially after the wet season, with cattle, random goat herds, donkey caravans, and wandering villagers all using the narrow roads. We decide to fly.

The short flight shows off the magnificence of the Rift Valley in the muted morning light. It is the world's greatest geographic trench, carving its way from Lebanon to Mozambique. We finally bump our way down the runway to the terminal. Harar was known as the 'City of Saints', boasting three mosques dating from the tenth century, and it subsequently emerged as a centre for Islamic culture. In the sixteenth century, a four-metre-high protective wall was built around the settlement and the town became known as Harar Jugol (fortified Harar). It became a major centre for commerce, linking African trade routes with the Red Sea and Arabia. Markets were set up at each of its five gates, trading incense, livestock, coffee, basil,

and woven baskets, but the most lucrative trade was, and still is, the narcotic plant khat (prounced chat).

Intrepid British explorer Sir Richard Burton, disguised as an Arab, maintained that Harar was the birthplace of khat, no doubt sampling its delights whilst communing with Hararians. Noted French poet Arthur Rimbaud, who had shocked nineteenth-century society with his decadent lifestyle, chose to live his final years in Harar, where they say he found peace (and probably the chewing of khat would have helped calm his restless soul).

Khat is an addictive narcotic, used by young and old in the horn of Africa and throughout Yemen. Families gather together to chew it and sip ginger tea at the day's end, but many become severely addicted. Overuse of the drug causes rotting teeth, hallucinations and psychosis. Stagnant economies and slow development in this area can be attributed to the ingrained khat culture.

Our amicable taxi driver winds through the tree-lined streets of Harar, past the imposing and ancient town wall, which makes the Old Town feel cozy and protected. Hotel Belayneh sits in poll position overlooking the Shoa Gate market but seems to be in the 'bare budget' category, judging by its state of disrepair. We were told this is the best place in Harar to view the markets.

Our bedroom has a small balcony just above the market-place so we can sit and watch it all happening below. The bed looks comfortable, with clean linen sheets, but there is no air-conditioning, so we hope Harar's altitude of 600 feet will bring cool breezes at nightfall. There are concrete floors, and torn curtains dangle sadly from bent curtain rods. There is a loo without a seat, and the shower alcove has a pipe jutting from the wall, with no shower rose, but a bucket filled with water sits underneath the pipe.

The staff are delightful, friendly and helpful, and speak some English. We are told there's a water problem today, and no running water for the moment. In fact, this is a permanent problem in Harar, with nearby Lake Alemaya's water levels dangerously low and putrid, so the health of those living here is far more at risk than that of two fly-by-night travellers. Staff no doubt spin this yarn to all their hotel guests. It is just one of many problems they have trying to run a hotel without running water.

We walk down the stone stairway to the bar restaurant to order ginger tea. Locals are clustered around an ancient and crackling television set watching a soccer game, so the disciple instantly joins them. Soon we have new friends, and despite no common language, the soccer game sets the tone, with cheers and jeers ringing out every few minutes.

Tea is refreshingly strong, and we order *fetira*, the traditional Hararian breakfast dish of fried dough cooked with an egg and crisped in a frypan before honey is generously ladled on top. It is delicious.

The markets outside are being assembled for the day's trade, and brightly coloured umbrellas shade the lines of vendors setting up their wares. They are mainly Harari and Oromo women, wearing vividly colourful robes of red, purple and orange that contrast superbly with their ebony skin. Soft headscarves cover their hair but not their faces.

Huge mounds of luscious green plants are displayed, and we realise the Shoa market is one of the main khat markets

in Harar. The plants are picked at dawn and taken to market, often stacked in carts and pulled there by donkeys. Lines of trucks and utes are parked nearby, waiting to be filled with this bounty. The drivers will deliver the khat to Djibouti, 227 kilometres from Harar, from where it will be shipped across the Red Sea to Aden. Speed is the essence; khat must be consumed within forty-eight hours of picking to attain the maximum effect, and the shocking road toll on the Harar to Djibouti road is testament to this.

We wander around the market stalls, seeing baskets, firewood, sugar cane, perfume oils and coffee beans being briskly traded. I notice that the market women here are in control of the dealing and the money exchange, and wonder if the khat chewing tradition is keeping their menfolk at home. There is laughter and tremendous camaraderie between the women running the khat stalls, and it is obvious they know the going price, and have no intention of discounting today's harvest.

At dusk, Abubakr, or Abu for short, is our driver and host for the longstanding tradition of feeding hyenas by the city wall. Hyenas have a 500-year-old history in Harar, scavenging the streets clean every night by eating refuse and offal. This has spawned folklore, the belief they bring good luck and rid the town of bad spirits, or Djinns. The story goes that Muslim Saints convened on a mountaintop to resolve the problem of hyena eating their livestock, making a pact to feed them instead. This practical decision is woven with superstition, and every year the Saints pact is celebrated on the Day of Ashura, when wheat porridge is prepared for the hyena pack. If more than half is eaten there will be a bountiful harvest, less than

half means famine for the coming year. In 1960, a farmer began handfeeding the hyenas. Now up to twenty assemble every evening by a Jugol gate to be fed by his descendants, the so-called hyena men.

Abu leads us to a space by the wall where we crouch near buckets containing hunks of camel and donkey meat. The hyena men call and whistle, and slowly the pack leader lopes towards us from the shrubbery nearby, followed by her clan of about nine hyenas. Their slanted backs make the front legs look smaller than their back legs. They are solidly built with spotted markings on their fur and their faces are appealing and beautiful, putting paid to their ferocious reputation.

The dominant female waits a metre from the bucket of meat. When a hunk is offered to her, she jumps forward and takes it deftly from the hyena man, who softly talks to her. Then I am handed a stick about ten centimetres long, with meat attached to its pronged end. By this time, eight hyenas are in a circle around us, waiting their turn.

One approaches me and snaps the meat off the stick in a quick bite. We can hear the bones being crunched to bits by a set of very strong teeth. The disciple is next, the colour of his face matching the pallid stone wall. He stretches his arm out with his head in reverse, his stance in 'fright and flight' mode. A juvenile approaches him and snaps off the meat, but instead of retreating to eat, stays close by happily chomping away.

The whole clan is now being fed. They are used to the ritual, and know and obey the hyena men. There is no sense of fear or aggression from either the humans or the animals, and now even the disciple seems relaxed. After all the meat has gone, the

clan will roam the streets of Harar scavenging throughout the night until dawn. If you were to meet them, they would ignore you and continue on their way.

The call to prayer resounds from mosque to mosque, with tenor, alto and falsetto tones, all vying for prominence, but it's a mis-matched orchestra that summons believers to face Mecca and pray. We return to the Belayneh for *injera* with spicy meat sauce, taken with local beer. Later, with our bedroom windows wide open, the cool breezes of the high altitude flow through, bringing relief from the heat of the day and allowing sleep.

Kondudo, a tabletop mountain with a thirteen-hectare grassy plateau, is home to East Africa's only feral horses, now numbering only ten or so. This decline in numbers has attracted British and Italian ecological groups keen to conserve them by working with National Parks of Ethiopia to promote tourism in the area. The monetary gain from tourism is benefiting locals, and giving them a reason to protect the feral horses.

Abu takes the wheel for the fifty-three-kilometre drive to Kondudo early in the morning so we can watch sunrise from its tabletop summit and observe the feral horses in their isolated habitat. A mist shrouds the landscape, with a pinky sky above promising a new day. Skilful driving by Abu has us on the plateau in under an hour from Harar.

A mare with two colts seems unperturbed by our presence. Other horses further away are silhouetted against the pink sky. Kondudo feral horses are descendants of domesticated horses abandoned here around 200 years ago. Flourishing Kondudo herds supplied Emperor Haile Selassie with horses for his personal stables in Addis Ababa.

The vast Horn of Africa is spread around us, and a spellbinding silence adds to the magnificence of the rising sun, broken by a whinny and neighing as the colts playfully jostle each other. They are a powerful symbol, demonstrating the resilience of all inhabitants, human and animal, that we have met in the Harar region of Ethiopia.

Catholics and Protestants in Belfast (1968)

True religion is the life we live, not the creed we profess

J.F. WRIGHT

'Girls, trade publicity want you to man the Australian stand at the Royal Ulster Show in Belfast next week,' says Blair Cook, manager and chaperone of the Golden Girls employed by Australia House in London. 'Please wear your mustard suits for a media call at Heathrow tomorrow, and be there at 10 am sharp! You will have two days to get to know Belfast before the show opens.' She continues with a detailed briefing of our exhibit duties before we are dismissed.

The Royal Ulster Show is Northern Ireland's major agricultural show, taking place in May every year. I embark on a flurry of activity, carefully packing uniforms and hats, a hairdryer complete with rollers and cap, packets of kangaroo pins, spare tights, and my Instamatic camera.

A trade attaché meets us at Heathrow, and we are introduced to the journalists who will cover the Ulster Show for the *Daily Express* and the *Daily Telegraph*, and some will accompany us on the flight. The attaché addresses the press: 'Australia House is sending their Golden Girl team to be hostesses on the Australian stand and the girls will be giving out samples of our produce to the public over the three day event.'

The journalists, all male, seem to be more interested in

surveying the sea of femininity in front of them than hearing about reasons for the journey, and the attaché seems rather peeved not to be part of our delegation but wishes us well as we board the plane. During the flight some fraternising with the journalists, promises some follow-ups and fun in Belfast.

A small private hotel, close to Queen's University, will be digs for Giz, Marg and myself, the rest of the team will stay at O'Kanes pub nearby. We hear that Queen's is harbouring an undercurrent of student disquiet over discrimination against Catholics in Northern Ireland, a divide that has ebbed and flowed over the centuries, but currently is really flowing.

The hotel's maitre d' is a formidable woman of a certain age, who greets us at the door and promptly delivers the rules of the hotel, including the horrifying news that there is just one bathroom and no showers. 'I have yet to discover a shower in the UK,' I hiss to Marg, who resignedly agrees. We wonder if the Irish are as hygienically challenged as the English, who seem to favour ablutions only once a week.

Miss McQuade is actually a delightful character, and at the end of her diatribe, invites us for a wee dram of Irish whisky, over which we hear about rumblings of trouble in the Falls Road area, and discover that Belfast is completely divided into Protestant and Catholic sectors. She is Protestant, and we are in a Protestant neighbourhood.

'Call me Maeve', she says, and there is a sharp rap at the back door. She jumps up. 'Ah, but that would be Kevin!' and opens the door to a policeman. Kevin hugs her and says, 'I'm free until five.'

It turns out that Kevin is one of few Catholic members of the Royal Ulster Constabulary, the almost exclusively Protestant

police force in Ulster. He has been Maeve's 'special friend' for years. Their relationship is a secret, even though they seem happy to reveal it to us. I sense he has broken away from a rigid Catholic relationship or marriage, and has found comfort in the Protestant arms of the opposing side, away from peering eyes.

We sit enthralled by Kevin's account of Belfast today, and hear that the current unrest is over the lack of housing for Catholics, and that jobs are denied to Catholics in favour of Protestants. Nearby, Shankhill Road is Protestant territory. 'Peace walls' of iron and barbed wire separate the communities, Catholic taxi drivers restrict themselves to Catholic sectors, and Protestant taxi drivers just work Protestant streets.

The government fears, with sound reasoning, that the Catholic Falls Road sector is controlled by Sinn Fein (associated with the Irish Republican Army). Reverend Ian Paisley, the Protestant firebrand, is inciting unrest almost every night on the television news. He leads the Loyalists, supporting Ulster's Protestant British government, and is opposed to the civil rights movement, which he sees as Southern Ireland's push to overtake Ulster and drown Protestants in Catholicism.

And here we have Kevin and Maeve, a harmonious example of mixing religions, albeit under cover. Giz asks if Kevin would show us the Falls Road, and he is happy to take us there. We pile into his police car to drive the ten minutes to Falls Road, where rundown tenements with narrow side alleys and no pavements give the impression we are in another country after the serene loveliness of the parks around Queen's. The Republic of Ireland flag flies over many buildings, and loitering youths are grouped together, with cigarette smoke wafting into the night air.

'No work for them, and no hope of it either,' says Kevin as

we swing back towards the university as Kevin responds to a call to return to headquarters. 'I'll drop you off at a pub near Queens.' We stop by a pub and step into a crowd of students, an overflow from inside. A band is playing, the music muted by the noise of patrons. We head for the bar queue, and Marg says, 'Let's try a Guinness!' Her accent attracts attention from a group behind us, who invite us to join them. There follows an evening of Irish indoctrination that we are only too happy to join, with fey descriptions in lilting accents embellishing every aspect of life, and mentions of Oliver Cromwell, Valera, and concern over the Parade of Orangeman in July.

Unbelievably, this concern refers to an event in 1690 AD, when Prince William of Orange defeated the Catholic King James in the Battle of the Boyne, between Dublin and Belfast. The victory established the Orange Order as a masonic-style brotherhood of Protestants, based in Northern Ireland, to uphold the faith. This 1690 AD victory is celebrated every July, with Orangemen donning bright orange sashes and waving the Orange Order flags as they march through the Catholic areas of Belfast. One could say 'only the Irish', but this tradition has been perpetuated for 300 years. I gather our new Irish friends are Protestant, but for us it is impossible to tell, as Irish looks, accents, and vivacity are the same wherever you are in Ireland.

As Australians, we are welcomed as long lost cousins. They all seem to have relatives living in Australia; some migrated during the Potato Famine of the mid 1800s. Their passion towards Ireland and its history seems clouded by a conviction that something must be done to rattle the bones of Westminster, before the current time bomb explodes.

Walking back to Maeve's hotel, we wonder if the turbulent

history of Ireland encourages cultural rites and superstitions, the passion for poetry and music and hero worship of legendary Irishmen. Perhaps it is their way of countering the oppressive control of religious dogma, or the gouging of Ireland's resources by British landlords. There's more than a whiff of change in the air, with the new contraceptive pill being taken by young Catholic women, who refuse to allow the church to rule their sex lives. The effect of 'swinging' London is evident here at the pub, with beehive hairdos, miniskirts, and dolly makeup.

Our last day is spent trekking around the foothills of the Mountains of Mourne, riding gentle old hacks from a local riding school, and taking in the stunning beauty of the Irish countryside. Tiny fields are enclosed by dry-stone walls, and farmhouses resemble cottages for the little people of *Gulliver's Travels*. Where the trail meets the ocean, we see a smuggler's cove from the 1800s, where tobacco, spirits and spices were collected from ships and taken by donkey along this path, known as the 'Brandy Pad'.

A pre Ulster Show reception will be held at O'Kanes, where the rest of our team are staying. The Irish press will attend, as well as the dishy media males from London we met at Heathrow. There are about sixty guests, many hovering around Giz, who charms with her Hungarian–Australian English, sparkling beaded cardigan and shiny black hair. Marg is statuesque in black, with fake opera-length pearls looking a million dollars, her porcelain skin is glowing after the day's Mountains of Mourne trek. I am aiming for a Jean Shrimpton look, but it's more healthy Aussie than London waif. There is music, platters of savouries and Babycham, an unbelievably popular fizzy sweet wine.

Trisha had misjudged the time, cutting short her ablutions to be punctual for Blair and the receiving line for the reception. The next morning we hear that the only bathroom at O'Kanes is in the attic and, in her haste, Trisha forgot to turn off the bath taps. At the party's close at midnight, she was greeted by waves of water gushing down the staircase. Trisha and Pam woke the night porter and bribed him to clear up the mess with one of our prize sample bottles of St Agnes Brandy VSOP. He promptly drank the whole bottle, and was found prostrate at the foot of the stairs the next morning by the hotel manager. The sodden carpets did not seem to worry him. 'Ah, they'll dry off today, and wasn't it a great party,' was his response.

We assemble at King's Hall, the venue for the Royal Ulster Show. The Australian stand has five podiums around its perimeter, so we stand three feet above the floor offering free samples of Ardmona peaches and pears, and Ambrosia rice in little sample saucers with tiny plastic spoons. This causes quite a sensation, with comments like: 'Come and see the Australian Aborigines', and 'Do you speak English, dear?'. It is quite clear that Australia is a complete unknown to most of the attendees, but overall the atmosphere is fun, and locals are curious about us, and about Australia.

There are mounds of Granny Smith apples in the centre of the stand, and a model of a merino sheep boasting a luxuriant woollen fleece is surrounded by lambskin rugs. Australian wines and spirits are well represented, but there are no tastings (it is thought the alcoholics of Belfast would bleed us dry) – speaking of which, our ambassador visits to officially open the stand, already well fuelled as he lurches from podium to podium reacquainting himself with the Golden Girls. His stoic

wife is not present, so it is up to Blair to take control. She looks like the Queen Mother in her pale-blue silk suit and matching hat, and she escorts our ambassador back to his car after the proceedings are over.

The three days of Show duty are filled with Irish fun and laughter, generosity and mischief, and leave an indelible impression that life is for living the Irish way, I could think of no better creed.

Postscript

9 October 1968: 2000 students from Queen's University marched in protest against police brutality in Belfast.

12 August 1969: The Battle of Bogside started as a riot in Derry. Eight people killed and 750 injured before it quickly spread to Belfast and throughout Northern Ireland. This was the beginning of a thirty-year civil war, with the British Army deployed and a death toll of 3523.

The Good Friday Agreement, an end to the Troubles, was reached in 1998.

Zanzibar (2005)

When you play the flute in Zanzibar,
all of Africa sings

ZANZIBAR PROVERB

Our backpacking son Barney has left Cape Town and is heading for Cairo. As we are also in Africa he suggests we make a side trip to meet him in Dar es Salaam, where he plans a two-day pause before trekking north. He directs us to meet him at a backpackers lodge in central Dar.

Expecting to be way out of the backpackers' age bracket, we jostle through the streets, milling with traders, spruikers and touts, and find an alley leading to the lodge. A Harley-Davidson motorbike takes pride of place in the courtyard, with six bicycles propped against the wall, and a green-and-white-tiled arched entrance leading to reception.

A corpulent Indian manager ticks off our names from a dog-eared book and says, 'Barney has arrived, mudum,' his bulbous black eyes hooded by heavy lids giving him an air of authority. 'He wanted to buy buttled water for your room, and will be back shortly.'

We walk up concrete steps to a room with two bunk beds and a mattress on the floor between them. An open window looks out to the street of noisy markets and a light sea breeze tempers the heat – but not the smell of curry and spice mixed with exhaust fumes from the belching traffic below.

Barney bursts into the room with six bottles of water and,

after hugs, tears and everyone talking at once, we go downstairs to the dining room for a late breakfast and a chance to hear about his adventures. So far, they have included his wallet being stolen from his jean's back pocket, endless driving in the back of a truck, burst tyres, border hold-ups, mozzies, a cobra, and tricky human personalities. 'It is always the foreigners and tourists who cause trouble, never the locals,' he says. Overall, the Africans with their friendliness and generosity, and the wonders of beautiful Africa, have trumped any of his problems en route.

The dining room is scattered with people, and sliced mango and papaya and hearty bacon and eggs are on offer by Bantu staff. The doors and windows are opened wide, with the high courtyard walls muting the noise of the streets outside.

The Harley Davidson couple, 1960s relics of the hippy era, are wearing leathers and T-shirts emblazoned with 'Wild Thing' and 'Che Guevara'. Grey lanky hair is fringed for madam, and a skinny ponytail, gathered from a balding pate, is the style for monsieur. A group of neat Germans in their forties sit together, and a melodramatic French group takes coffee in the courtyard, with '*Alors!*' and '*Tres difficile!*' peppering their conversation.

Dar es Salaam, meaning 'residence of peace' in Arabic, is affectionately called 'Dar' by locals. In the mid-nineteenth century it was a fishing village, but with the emergence of colonists – first the Germans, and then the British – its strategic position on East Africa's coast, and proximity to Zanzibar, made it the central hub for trade in spices, ivory and the traffic of slaves to Arabia.

We spend two memorable days with Barney, fossicking through local markets to find indigenous handwork in leather

and textiles, usually made by women and depicting their individual village traditions and lifestyle. I find an exquisite wall hanging of African village life, embroidered in bright colours on a turquoise backing with chooks, children, huts and campfires all embossed in naive art style. Spicy curries, delicious kebabs, and pita bread wrapping meat sauces, are a combination of the Arab, Indian and African cuisine that has been in the cultural mix of Dar since the mid 1800s.

Barney's truck of backpackers departs early for Kenya. He now has a sealed capsule for his valuables hanging securely around his neck, his jeans and T-shirts have been laundered, and energy bars are stuffed into any available space.

He is more than ready to embrace the next chapter of adventures.

The fast ferry to Zanzibar is within walking distance of the lodge, so we pull our wheelie bags to the Port between the market stalls being set up for the day's business. Shady trees line the boulevard nearby, with bursts of orange and magenta of bougainvillea hedges in flower, their vivid fronds twining into the lower branches.

The disciple has a sturdy stomach at sea, but I'm known to be seasick sailing over ripples, so I take up position at the stern of the ferry with firm hands clasping the railings, and focus my eyes on the horizon. We take off with a swoosh of speed, and plane over the swells and dips in the two-hour passage to Zanzibar. It is exhilarating, pleasantly warm, and the speed seems to dispel any nausea – although the final ten minutes of choppy sea puts paid to that, and I am very happy to disembark.

Zanzibar in Persian comes from 'Zangh Bar', meaning 'Negro Coast' or, in Arabic, 'Zayn Z'al' meaning 'fair land'.

Both are considered authentic. For centuries, Zanzibar has been a trading post between Africa, Arabia and India, and eventually became part of the Sultanate of Oman, where the ruling Arab elite used the Bantu general population as their workers until Independence in 1963. Zanzibar and the surrounding islands were known as the Spice Islands, with lucrative trade in spices and ivory from elephants killed in neighbouring Tanganyika.

It was also a major hub for the East African slave trade, and with the abolition of slavery in 1890 Zanzibar became a British Protectorate. However, following the death of Sultan Hamad in 1896, a cousin of the Sultan took control, keen to continue the lucrative slave market. The British responded by declaring war on Zanzibar; Royal Navy ships opened fire from the bay. The cousin promptly fled to the German Consulate and a ceasefire was declared. The Anglo–Zanzibar war lasted forty-five minutes, making this the shortest war in history. The new Sultan Hamoud acquiesced to British demands, and brought an end to the slave trade by barring slavery and freeing the slaves.

We find a taxi driver happy to take us to Matemwe, an hour's drive from the port and located on the north-eastern coast of Zanzibar. We drive through farming countryside with Farid, our driver, knowledgeable about spices after a childhood spent on a spice farm. 'The queen of spice is vanilla,' he says, 'because each bush must be hand pollinated by the farmer, and when the pods grow they are boiled and then sun dried, ready for market.' Cloves are an important export, and were Zanzibar's major crop in the 1800s, with the port warehouses so crammed with the spice that on entering the harbour you could smell cloves in the air. Cinnamon comes from the bark of a laurel tree, and is used as a digestive, and a cure for colds,

as well as being a delicious cooking additive. There are legends, superstitions and health remedies attached to every spice, with cardamom, turmeric, nutmeg, black pepper and lemon grass all grown in this area. I feel like riding in Farid's taxi with my head stretched out the window to deeply inhale the intoxicating scents that hover over the spice farms as we drive.

Matemwe is accessed by narrow dirt roads, and the beach hut accommodation we choose has a mud-brick reception and dining area, and a thatched roof. The amiable Abdul leads us to a pristine white beach rimming the turquoise Indian Ocean, where six little beach huts sit on the sand. Our hut of coconut palm leaves dried and woven to construct the walls and roof is completely open to the elements. There are two beds inside, with mozzie nets draped over each, and there's a loosely latched door to allow the sea breeze in, and flutter the nets seductively. Imagine walking on pristine white sand into your simple shelter, listening to the gentle lapping of the sea just twenty metres away. It makes me think of desert island myths. This is a rare find on an island that has become a tourist mecca with ostentatious resorts.

We walk along the sand finding shells and come across a small fishing village, nestled in the shrubbery. Here we meet Mussa, who is untangling fishing nets by a '*ngalawa*', or traditional Zanzibar fishing canoe. The *ngalawa*, gouged from a mango tree, is around eighteen-feet long with two masts and sugar sacks to serve as sails.

Mussa speaks good English, and we discover his livelihood relies on fishing for octopus, with cockles and shellfish a sideline. I ask if he would allow us to go fishing with him, and he smiles broadly and agrees to do so for some American dollars,

he will provide us with masks and fins so we can snorkel while he fishes. 'Be at the village by 9 am, as we need to catch the tide to safely cross the atoll,' he says.

The pink sky at dusk, the gentle warmth, scent of frangipani and sound of crickets sets a soporific mood for gin and tonics, followed by eye-watering curries. There is a low occupancy here, which adds to the magic of feeling isolated in paradise. The gentle lapping of waves is our night's background music as we lie later in our beach hut.

We meet Mussa at 9 am with Jamal, his fishing partner. The snorkels and fins are put under the canoe-shaped bow, and there is a huge coconut, a lethal-looking African *pangar* (knife), and their fishing equipment filling the stern. We push the *ngalawa* into the ocean and all climb aboard. Jamal sets the sails and a breeze gently fills them, while Mussa strongly rows towards the atoll. 'Just in time!' he says.

We need high tide to cross the reef, and do so without scraping the hull before sailing past the point to the open sea. Stronger breezes fill the sails and Mussa can rest his arms from rowing. 'We are heading for an island and I shall anchor off-shore,' he says. 'There are wonderful tropical fish for you to see while Jamal and I fish.'

I dive in after the anchor has secured the boat, the disciple follows. The water is warm, clear and the most remarkable turquoise colour. Mussa is right about the fish, every size shape and colour can be seen in schools of yellow and black striped, red and silver, gold and green. It's a natural aquarium that mesmerises and compels us to stay and watch for more.

The island is about 200 metres away and is a 7-star luxury getaway for the mega-rich. We see security guards patrolling

the exquisite beach entirely devoid of guests. 'Let's swim to shore to take a break!' I say to the disciple. And we do so, but are immediately told to return to the sea by a guard delighted to have something different to do with his day, to exercise his authority. We return to Mussa and Jamal, and as it is quite a long swim back to the boat we need much help to clamber aboard.

'Time for lunch,' Mussa says. And with that he pierces a hole in the coconut and we all take a turn to drink the delicious and reviving milk. Then with a swing of his *pangar* he cuts the coconut into two and then four pieces, and we have a lunch of delicious succulent coconut. A crate full of writhing octopus sits plumb centre in the *ngalawa*'s hull, it's been a good day's catch.

Mussa gets Jamal to set sail. We need to pace ourselves to catch the tide in order to cross the atoll in time to get back to Matemwe. There is little wind and much rowing, but when the boat starts to cross the reef, there is the ominous sound of scraping, causing concern for Mussa. Suddenly a large wave appears from behind and the boat surfs over the reef with a whoosh, and we are safe. The wind then picks up, allowing a gentle sail around the point without oars, and we continue sailing all the way to Matemwe.

Dhow Drifting in Oman (2013)

An ancient dhow with billowing sails
Mimes the dance of the seven veils
When breezes blow, when breezes blow

H.L. CADDICK

I think of vaudeville costumes from the Folies Bergère on entering the Muttrah Souk to see local women tented in black choosing dresses from vibrantly coloured satins and silks with sequinned bodices, ruffles, and finished in gold thread. Oh, how I would love to see them cavort in this finery at home, behind their high walls!

There is a pungent smell of spice, and incense burns at most stalls that line the ancient arched malls of the souk. Perfume oils can be mixed to satisfy any whim or fancy. Most perfume sellers boast that they have mastered the art of reproducing French perfumes, so I order Chanel No 5, and the result is not bad for $15. The mixture is dripped carefully into an Arabic perfume bottle with a golden tassel tied around the glass stopper.

Muscat has been a trading hub for centuries, linking East Africa and Zanzibar to Arabia, Central Asia, and beyond with spices, ivory and, until 1890, the slave trade providing a treasure trove for Omanis. The port of Muscat, guarded by a romantically turreted fort, lies opposite the souk, so there's a sense of

adventure walking through these alleyways – I wouldn't be surprised to see Aladdin appear from behind an architrave.

We fly to Khasab, the main town on the Musandam Peninsula in far northern Oman, where the Strait of Hormuz allows a narrow entry into the Persian Gulf. A complex series of pristine fjords in Musandam has enticed us to take a dhow trip to this natural wonderland that now has World Heritage listing.

It is late afternoon and the pilot descends the prop-engined plane to just above a golden-orange range of barren mountains and, with a final downward swoop, through a narrow valley to the runway. He taxis to a remote building that seems to have no staff on duty, and the terminal doors are closed.

We are the only foreigners, the eight other passengers have families or cars meeting them On taking our bags from the trolley beside the plane we realise there will be no taxis, and we might need to walk into the town. By luck, the pilot walks past us, having just signed off, and offers a lift. As the call to prayer echoes from mosque to mosque, he finally pulls up at our little hotel and bids us farewell.

The Indian manager rushes out apologising for not meeting us at the airport. 'Did you know the cricket is on in Karachi,' he says, 'and Australia is all out for 200?' He is talking the disciple's language, and cricket dominates the conversation over iced mango juice. Afterwards, Mohamed hands us the keys to his car so we can investigate the port before nightfall.

Dodging herds of goats and general populace through Khasab's narrow streets, we reach the port to see lines of speedboats from Bandar Abbas loading their contraband of smuggled cigarettes, mobile phones and computers into crates before

setting off across the Persian Gulf. Bandar Abbas, on Iran's southern coast, is just a short hop from Khasab. This trade continues without censure, no doubt because palms have been greased, and a percentage of the profits have been spread about to everyone's satisfaction.

Dhows are being attended to in a nearby marina, with fishing hauls piled high on deck. The day's catch is being sold with loud and dramatic interaction between the fishermen and shopkeepers. We find a dhow that will take us on a cruise around Musandam, its captain, another Mohamed, is mending a sail. 'Be here at 8 am,' he says, a cigarette dangling from the corner of his mouth as he names his price. The dhow is carpeted with rugs and the divans around the hull are upholstered and invitingly cushioned. There is a central stove positioned by the main mast for cooking, and snorkels and fins are stacked in a plastic crate to the side. Mohamed's craggy face breaks into a grin, the cigarette still well lodged, as he waves us goodbye with promises of an unforgettable day to come.

The following morning we are welcomed on board like family members. Yusuf and yet another Mohamed are crew; we are the only guests, and must remove our shoes before walking on the plush carpet that covers the deck. We recline on divans bolstered by comfy cushions as Arabian coffee is served with fresh dates.

A guttural engine vibrates and the dhow chugs beyond the marina and past the breakwater to open sea. Mohamed cuts the engine. Strong winds are filling the sails. Before long the timbers creak and the sails flap and whitecaps spray behind us as the dhow slices through waves along the coast towards Musandam's entrance. We sail along the giant fjord Khor-Sham, cormorants

circling above and an eagle watching us from his eerie on the cliff top. A pod of dolphins surface, and play in the wake before deciding to compete with the dhow, and soon there are three dolphins each side of the bow, their leader out in front showing us the way.

A turtle slowly paddles by, his head lifted like a periscope, and flying fish skim the water, their silver bodies reflecting the sun's rays.

We stop at a small bay and drop anchor. It is hot and still, but the sails cast shade over the deck, and the silence is broken only by a soft lap of ripples against the rocks. Mohamed starts cooking and throwing spices over lamb and chicken pieces as they sizzle on a frypan, while Yusuf boils rice in a lidded tin pot.

'It's a bit hot for curry!' I whisper to the disciple, as we put on fins and goggles and dive overboard. We hope to swim with the dolphins but they have disappeared, so we spend hours lying prone, buoyed by the seawater. Our goggles reveal a wonderland of coral reefs and shells with multi-coloured fish darting around, and seaweed gently swaying from the tide's ebb and flow. It is both mesmerising and addictive. We finally clamber aboard the dhow and find the hot curries are reviving and welcome, despite the heat.

Mohamed pulls anchor and we set sail for Telegraph Island, further along the fjord. The island is really an islet of small dimensions, with the ruins of British Telegraph Officers's quarters on a small hill in the centre of the outpost surrounded by fertile reefs and limpid rock pools. Telegraph Island served as a booster station for the first telegraphic cable between London and Karachi, and is credited with the term 'round the bend',

being the result of officers maddened by the heat and isolation being desperate to go 'round the bend' of the fjord, and back to civilisation.

We spend the afternoon snorkelling around the island and bathing in the rock pools, with the two Mohameds and Yusuf happily fishing and smoking together on the dhow. The pod of dolphins rejoins us in the late afternoon as we head for home. They escort the dhow, leaving us where the fjord meets with the Gulf, a perfect climax to the day.

Strong winds set a cracking pace, with the sails fully extended to maximise speed and exhilaration. We meet a line of speed-boats racing across the Gulf, with their latest haul of contraband bound for Bandar Abbas. Then, slowly we enter Khasab's port and dock, just as local fishermen are unloading their day's catch ready for the evening markets.

Pamukkale, Konya and Cappadoccia by Bus (1989)

I'd rather go by bus!

PRINCE CHARLES

We have almost circled this vast country on local buses 'en famile' on our cheap and cheerful holiday in Turkey. So I can sing my praises to the Turkish bus culture, and at around five dollars each for a four-hour journey it fits our limited budget.

There are a few ground rules to consider: never travel at night, due to the accident statistics; always sit close to the front for a panoramic view; choose the newest bus from the assortment parked at the bus station; and, finally, expect the unexpected.

We have survived a bus race between two macho bus drivers on a narrow road heading for Van, both buses filled with passengers and our driver ignoring shouts for him to slow down.

On another trip, lack of snow chains on the bus tyres caused a slide over against a mountainside close to the Russian border, prompting an army rescue and recuperation at their outpost quarters. There have been near misses on the road involving trucks, herds of sheep, and donkey carts, but for some reason we tend to be fatalistic about it all, and are ready for our next sortie, from Izmir to Pamukkale – because travelling by bus in Turkey is fun!

The bus station at Izmir is bursting with travellers, but being wintry December, they are local Turkish families or businessmen; the tourists must be waiting for summer.

The bus company touts are shouting their prices and selling tickets to customers, who then queue to board the buses, parked in parallel lines, with destination plaques on their windscreens The baggage holds are open, and the drivers chain smoke as they chat with passengers, always willing to lift bags, cartons and cases into the hold, bowing greetings to women and the aged, and joking with children.

It is cold and wintry, and the salep stall is doing a brisk business. This sweet, hot and glutinous drink helps fend off the cold. Turkish women board our bus with bags of strongly smelling salami and bread rolls to eat en route, and large sacks of produce bought at the markets that they stuff under seats or in any overhead luggage space. The bus smells like a market stall.

We take the four front seats split in two by the aisle. It's like being in a receiving line, with every Turkish passenger greeting us with '*Gunaydin!*' (good morning) and either tweaking Barney's cheeks and ruffling his red hair, or offering Toby sweets for the journey. The windscreen is bordered with fringes and tassels and the ubiquitous evil eye hangs above the driver's seat as a deterrent to bad luck.

We are now used to speakers being turned to maximum volume for the Turkish music that will play for the entire journey, and I bless the Nintendo, Donkey Kong and Pac-Man gadgets the boys carry with them,, which keep them occupied on this four-hour bus trip

The bus is now full, and our driver jumps aboard with a

swagger and stubs his cigarette into an already full ashtray by the steering wheel. He is well in command wearing a black-leather bomber jacket with trendy sunglasses despite the dull-grey morning sky. He revs the idling engine a few times, like a plane getting ready for take off, but we depart slowly, succumbing to the pace of traffic in Izmir. We eventually emerge to the open road and he plants his foot hard on the accelerator and soon the speed dial registers 130 kph. Then the Eastern music is turned on, the type that accompanies belly dancing. The windscreen fringes dance and sway, and I'm hoping the evil-eye charm will work its magic for us once more as we speed ahead. The boys are focusing on their games, and we are taking in the enormity and beauty of the Turkish countryside when, after about an hour of driving, Barney and I have a brisk exchange: 'Why didn't you go at the bus station?'

'I didn't need to!'

'I can't ask the bus driver to stop!'

"You have to, Mum!'

So, the bus pulls over to the side, the driver is not pleased as he opens the door, and we see a 'Mannekin Pis' rendition in the snowy Turkish landscape as the driver drums his fingers on the steering wheel, marking time. The speeding seems to increase after this little incident and, finally, passing through Denzili we reach Pamukkale in the early afternoon.

Pamukkale means 'cotton castle' in Turkish. It is a remarkable 200-metre-high cliff of dazzling white pool formations. These thermal waters have been sought-after for their therapeutic virtues and miracle cures for centuries. The terraced basins are known as travertines, and are formed from the calcium carbonate residue left behind as hot water gushes from

our planet's heart. There are petrified waterfalls, and stalactites that are constantly renewed and whitened by this process. It is quite extraordinary to view this 'cotton castle' in the mellow light of late afternoon.

The Romans favoured this area as a spa retreat, and 2000 years later nothing much has changed. There is a complex series of canals bringing thermal water to surrounding villages and fields of Pamukkale. Our hotel lies adjacent to the cliff, and is built around a large thermal pool that flows into small canals with bridges allowing access to the hotel bedrooms. There are Roman columns submerged in the main pool, ruptured during an earthquake and now used as a place to sit while immersed in the waters. Steam is permanently hovering over the 35°C water, a nice contrast to this wintry day of 3°C, and being winter there are few guests. We wallow in the blissfully hot water, with the strange sensation of the freezing-cold air above us.

A German gentleman is loudly lecturing a small travel group in dogmatic German, explaining the process and protocols of spas and comparing Pamukkale with Baden Baden in Germany. It amazes me that they all dutifully listen, and there follows a ritual of sluicing the arms first, then the head, and I hold the startlingly depressing view that many people would rather obey process than abandon themselves to the beauty and freedom of such an experience.

The other guests are Italian. Silvio is wallowing and completely oblivious to his wife's melodramatic calls to join her in the canal. '*Silvio, Silvio, vieni con me, vieni con me!*'

The boys have found goggles and dive down to explore the Roman column, while the disciple lies on his back gazing at the heavens above where, obligingly, a full moon shines a

ghostly light on the Taurus mountains in the distance. I would happily spend hours in this hot water but finally, with our fingers crinkled by the long session, we all grab towels and run through freezing temperatures to our room, trying not to slip on the tiles.

The ruins of Hierapolis lie behind Pamukkale and are a short walk from the hotel. The city was established in the second century BC as a thermal spa by the Attalid Kings of Pergamon. Later, when ceded to Rome, it became a religious centre for the Eastern Roman Empire.

There is a magnificent amphitheatre, used in summer for performances, but being winter the amphitheatre is ours alone as the boys test the acoustics and jump down the tiers of stone. Hierapolis now has UNESCO World Heritage status.

Walking over the fields behind Hierapolis, we see sheep grazing, and a small shelter half embedded into the hillside. It is a shepherd's home, and he quickly approaches and beckons us to come inside. The main room is cosy and warm and his wife is sitting on the rugs on the floor among exquisitely embroidered scarves, placemats and tablecloths spread out in neat piles. They are for sale. It is customary to bargain, and if you bargain well and with good manners you gain respect. So, with much humour and banter, we agree on prices, all through sign language, and then accept hot apple tea as a conclusion to the deal before bidding them farewell.

This handiwork is unfortunately a dying art in Turkey, with technology and a Westernised culture taking over from the gentle arts. Each province has a different style of embroidery, passed on through generations of women hand sewing together through the winter months, and selling their wares in summer.

The cotton voile scarves, embroidered and fringed, are used as head scarves for Eastern women, but can be used as table throws or neck scarves for those from the West.

We are split up on the bus to Konya, with the disciple sitting next to a local Turkish salesman who insists on paying for his fare, as a mark of traditional Turkish hospitality to a foreigner. During the seven-hour bus trip he provides sweets and snacks as well, ignoring offers to repay him for his generosity and kindness. 'We look after guests to our country,' he says and, to his delight, I find a kangaroo broach to pin on his lapel. We alight, wrapping woollen scarves around our necks and pulling on hats and gloves to combat the bitter cold of Konya.

In the twelfth century, Konya was Seljuk Turkey's capital, and the cultural centre for Anatolia. It is here that the mystic and poet Mevlana Rumi founded the sect of Whirling Dervishes. He professed to be open to all religions:

> 'I'm neither of the East or the West,
> No boundaries exist within my breast'

The annual Sama ceremony is famous for the dance of white-robed and cone-hatted dervishes, twirling in circles with their right arms extended to the heavens, linking them to earth, their left arms pointing to the floor. They are seeking to connect the divine with humanity.

An aged dervish gentleman, using a walking stick, whispers in reverence as we enter Rumi's mausoleum. This adds to the strong mystical sense felt in this ancient building, which adjoins the Medrese, Mosque and Dervish Dance Hall. Exquisite calligraphy on ancient manuscripts of Rumi's poems and teachings are displayed in glass cases, with wonderful quotes like:

'Let yourself be silently drawn by what you love, and you will not be lead astray.' The turmoil of commercial Konya outside is in stark contrast. Trucks, *dolmuş* mini-buses, and cars in gridlocked traffic, all the noise and bustle of today's world.

Urgup is in the heart of the moonscape that is Cappadoccia, and just three hours by bus from Konya. There is a thick covering of snow at 3000 feet as we pass the famous Fairy Chimneys or Hoodoos, where strong winds and rain over centuries have carved their conical shapes from the volcanic rock. It looks as if they've jumped out of a children's picture book, with their snowy caps glistening in the sun.

A central square in the little town of Urgup has carpet and antiquities bazaars and is a source for the best lapis lazuli, which finds it's way here from Afghanistan. Veined in gold the lapis is the darkest blue, and there are eggs, necklaces and carved Buddhas on sale, as well as ancient Persian samovars. The carpet seller has a different selection of kilims from those we've seen in Istanbul. The patterns and weaves tell stories of Central Anatolia with their colourful dyes a jealously guarded trade secret. We manage to resist buying yet another kilim, but proudly wander off with some beautiful lapis lazuli.

Cappadoccia has a maze of troglodyte villages, underground towns, churches and a cathedral dating back to the fourth century AD. Rock-hewn churches still display frescoes from the Crusades, and further back to Christian symbols from Roman times. The underground living began with Christian monks residing in the caves but later underground towns were carved out of the soft volcanic rock, and became the refuge for Christian populations during Arab invasions.

We stay at one of the many cave hotels in the area, feeling

part of this extraordinary history and lifestyle of living as a troglodyte and appreciating the cozy warmth of being underground, compared with the biting cold and snow outside.

We enjoy three days of exploring rugged up like Eskimos. We trudge through the snow, climbing into caves and through passageways to underground churches and troglodyte dwellings, and it feels as though we are living every era of ancient history. Cappadoccia is a memorable climax to this Anatolian adventure.

Etosha and Tracking Desert Elephants (2015)

People must feel that the natural world is important, wonderful, amazing and a pleasure

DAVID ATTENBOROUGH

Well at the moment I do not feel the natural world is wonderful, amazing, and a pleasure! It is 40°C and the disciple has managed to puncture two tyres at once swooping through a dry creek bed at high speed. We have limped to a standstill realising we are well and truly stuck on a lonely dust track between Namutoni and Halali in Namibia's Etosha pan. One tyre is successfully changed, but not having two spare tyres we have a problem. It is around midday, the lions are sleeping and the rustles we hear in the bush are more likely to be hornbills than anything more sinister. With the car doors open, we sit and wait and try to stay calm.

A cloud of dust signals an approaching car and a 'bakkie' (Africa's four-door ute) with a family of South Africans on board stops. Although they are heading for Namutoni they backtrack the ten kilometres to Halali with our two punctured tyres thrown on top of their camping gear in the back and the promise of a quick return.

This extraordinary generosity leaves us gobsmacked and faint with relief, but our expressions of gratitude are swept aside with, 'Man, you're Aussies, we love Aussies – ' and a pause

before, ' – except during cricket or rugby games. See you soon!'

Within the hour they return, and then continue on their original journey with hoots and waves. Behind them is another bakkie, driven by the Halali mechanic who deftly replaces the spare and attaches the second tyre, clicking off the jack and accepting a tip with a sheepish grin before he bids us to follow him to Halali.

Etosha, part of the Kalahari Basin in northern Namibia, is a large saltpan spreading over 4800 square kilometres and surrounded by dense Mopane woodland. Etosha means 'Great White Place'. The pan is mostly dry, but has waterholes favoured by a rich variety of wildlife. Legend has it that the sole survivor of a village raid created a massive lake with her tears of sorrow, and the sun eventually dried those tears to salt.

The Halali camp is a great pit stop after our adventure and, fully refreshed, we set off at a more demure pace for Okaukuejo just seventy kilometres down the road. Dazzles of zebra gallop across the track towards what looks like at least 300 zebra in the distance. It is now believed the zebras' black and white stripes create micro-thermals that serve to cool their bodies in the relentless heat of the African sun. Giraffe saunter by, or just stand still and stare as we pass; a solitary jackal weaves his way with intent. Vultures are circling above for carrion. Research has revealed that they are capable of seeing a six-centimetre object from a height of a kilometre.

Okaukuejo has a spectacular waterhole, famous for visits from diverse and plentiful wildlife, and we are allotted a rondavel close by. The rondavel is conically thatched and cool inside, with a ceiling fan gently moving the air over the bed and billowing the mozzie nets.

The camp is well appointed with shady trees shrouding a restaurant and swimming pool, a great place to relax after the heat and dust of game drives in the pan.

There is a petrol station and supermarket for campers, and a tourist shop selling locally made handcrafts. Rangers and staff are African Namibians from the Kalahari Basin area of Etosha This local employment is important for wildlife conservation, as their livelihood is dependent on Etosha being a fertile haven for endangered animals: to reap the rewards, they must conserve wildlife.

A blood-red sun drops below the horizon at the predicted time of 5.31 pm, and auras of pinks and purples remain in the sky. The waterhole has a thatched hide, tiered with stone slabs for seating, and is a perfect spot to view the passing parade of animals which, amazingly, seem to be in a queue, species by species. Impala, wildebeest, and a solitary jackal surround the waterhole and are drinking and sloshing about, with one wary eye watching for predators. Behind a shrubbery of acacias are six giraffe, grouped together and waiting their turn.

Every evening a herd of elephants time their arrival for around 7 pm, and can be seen in the far distance sauntering along as they make their approach. This family group of seven are being lead by the matriarch. Elephants do not wait their turn, but approach the water expecting all animals to vacate the premises, which of course they do, with the exception of the jackal sniffing around the water's edge. The matriarch, mother and aunties are nurturing a baby elephant of about three months old. The mother nudges him into the water with her trunk, gently pouring water over him, and then drawing more water through her trunk to splash over herself. A young adolescent

male is being trained in manners and curbed with a swift strike on the rump from the matriarch if he becomes too boisterous near the baby. The elephants stay for an hour or so and then are briskly summoned by the matriarch, who leads them past our hide and across to the Mopane woodland in the distance.

Muted floodlighting allows good visibility over the water-hole and does not seem to affect animal behaviour, but tonight we also have the light of a full moon, revealing a landscape of shadows and movement as more animals approach the water. A white rhino and calf are the next visitors, I estimate the baby to be about two months old. It is a special moment, as today this magnificent species is facing extinction due to unbridled poaching for rhino horn.

In 2015, it became a genocide, with one rhino killed every six hours in South Africa. Rhino horn is now worth $90,000 per kilo in South East Asian countries, where it is believed to be a remedy for curing all ills, from cancer and sexual impotence to hangovers. There are strong forces now trying to combat this problem, but it may be too late to save the species.

Rhinos love to wallow in mud. They tend not to swim about in the water like hippos, but drink their fill at the water's edge. The baby rhino stands close to his mother, and suddenly we see a male lion, eyes focused on the rhino baby, charging towards him from the acacia shrubbery. The female rhino snorts in fury, turns on a sixpence and charges the lion before he has a chance to attack the baby. Lions know that they cannot beat an adult rhino in speed or strength This young male lion yowls his frustration with the snorting rhino at his heels and manages to escape without being gored, obviously learning his first lesson about the futility of attacking rhinos. The mother returns to

her calf and they continue to drink at the water's edge. We feel privileged to have seen firsthand, one of life's many altercations in the wild.

A spotted eagle owl has a nest in the enormous leadwood tree behind the waterhole. These birds practice pair fidelity and mate for life. We wonder if the mate is still hunting while this beautiful creature guards the nest, her elegant silhouette outlined by moonlight. Each night spent at the waterhole reveals a continuing saga, where in the end only the strongest survive in the wild After years of driving on long safaris, I would say that finding a waterhole and staying put reaps more reward than driving for miles in the bush.

Twyfelfontein is in the Kunene region of Kalahari country. Here pre-historic volcanic activity coupled with wild weather has carved craters and weird rock formations. This desert landscape is also home to the fabled desert elephants.

The 300-kilometre gravel road from Okaukuejo has dry creek beds, jagged rocks and potholes and it is a daunting six-hour experience, with animated marital discussion over directions, coupled with sheer fatigue while concentrating on the road.

The Twyfelfontein Lodge is finally reached after a lucky right-hand turn on a forked road with no signpost. The lodge is built into a sheer cliff face of russet rocks that are carved and shaped like a *Star Wars* landscape and overlooks miles of desert terrain, sliced by dry riverbeds. The thatched visitor centre is accessed through a narrow pass that weaves through the rocks. It is a hub for tourist traffic to ancient rock carvings, as well as desert elephant tracking.

A rock pool converted for swimming is welcome relief to

frayed tempers, the heat and dust, and later anti-malarial gin and tonics taken on the centre's upper level puts all things right with the world. The enormous thatched roof has timber struts and covers a terrace overlooking a landscape as dramatic as Ngorongoro for its size and majesty, with red rock shapes and cliffs looking down on an endless expanse of desert plains.

Martin, our ranger, insists on an early start as it might take most of the day to track a herd of the elephants. We climb into his jeep at 7 am with gear necessary to survive the day crammed into a small backpack. Desert elephants have adapted to their dry and sandy habitat by developing a smaller body mass, larger feet, and longer legs than other elephants. During the dry season, they will eat roots of trees and dry grass as they follow traditional routes, digging holes or '*gorras*' along courses they know will deliver water. Elephants talk to each other using low frequency rumbles, undetectable to the human ear, but heard by other elephants fifty kilometres away.

Martin has been involved with desert elephant tracking for years, and regales us with stories as we speed along a narrow dirt track for over an hour before we enter the first dry riverbed. He slows the jeep as we scan the silt, looking for footprints or freshly broken branches of the Mopane trees that elephants love to eat. 'They've been here this morning!' he says with delight, and we see a mess of broken branches and footprints on the riverbank. He continues driving for ten kilometres to an adjacent sandy plain surrounded by artistically carved red rocks and there they are, at least fifteen elephants clustered together, bathing themselves in the red dust by using their trunks, the babies walking between their mother's legs and the matriarch leading the herd.

Suddenly two adolescent males turn and look at our jeep. They wave their heads from side to side, and then spread their ears into 'we shall charge' mode – and they do so, with frightening speed accompanied by the noise of attack, stopping just short of our bonnet. They stare at us, before turning away with snorts and trumpets of triumph. 'They were bluffing!' says Martin, 'and had we reversed they would have continued to pursue us and probably tried to overturn the jeep.'

We are still shaking and trying to recover some equilibrium, but are more then impressed with Martin's cool attitude. He restarts the engine, and continues to follow the herd, but at a safer distance, and although we might be unwanted observers of these incredible survivors, it is a privilege to have shared a day in their lives.

Postscript

In the early 1900s, there were 3000 elephants roaming the Kunene region of Namibia. In the past century, rampant poaching has reduced this number to around 800. Recently Namibia has established a Shire Conservancy that encourages locals to be employed and their communities to profit from tourism.

Slowly the situation is repairing, and through education, and receiving the benefits from tourism, they are learning the importance of protecting the elephants.

Epilogue

I started writing this book in 2015, a year punctuated by global terrorism. My hope is these travel stories will convince all who read it that human interaction is precious, enlightening and always possible, whatever the creed or culture.

Curiosity is the oxygen fuelling my travel adventures, with the constant thread of human kindness and generosity weaving through incidents and obstacles along the way. I encourage readers to keep their curiosity alive, and to always consider the road less travelled.

Also by Heather Caddick

For the Love of Rhinos (and this life)

Wakefield Press is an independent publishing and distribution company based in Adelaide, South Australia. We love good stories and publish beautiful books. To see our full range of books, please visit our website at www.wakefieldpress.com.au where all titles are available for purchase.

Find us!

Twitter: www.twitter.com/wakefieldpress
Facebook: www.facebook.com/wakefield.press
Instagram: instagram.com/wakefieldpress

CPSIA information can be obtained
at www.ICGtesting.com
Printed in the USA
BVOW05*1935011017
5985BVAU00001B/1/P

9 781743 054543